Surrogacy

A legal and practical guide for Queensland

By Elizabeth Fairon

First published 2024 by Elf Law Pty Ltd, Australia

Produced by Independent Ink

Cover design by Pixel Co Creative & Marketing & EM
Typeset in Bembo MT Pro by Post Pre-press Group, Brisbane

ISBN: 978-1-923249-05-9 (paperback)
ISBN: 978-1-923249-04-2 (kindle)

Love recognises no barriers. It jumps hurdles, leaps fences, penetrates walls to arrive at its destination full of hope.

–Maya Angelou

Contents

Introduction

Welcome to Surrogacy in Queensland, a comprehensive guide crafted to navigate surrogacy law and practice in Queensland, Australia. This book is your essential companion, offering clear, practical insights and case studies to empower both intended parents and birth parents throughout the surrogacy journey.

Surrogacy is a deeply personal and legally complex path to parenthood. In this book, you will find not only legal guidelines but also practical tips to help you manage every step – from initial considerations and medical preparations to birth registration and beyond.

Whether you are considering surrogacy as an intended parent or contemplating becoming a surrogate, this book equips you with the knowledge and tools necessary to make informed decisions and navigate the process with confidence. Our goal is to support you through the complexities of surrogacy, ensuring that every choice made is grounded in knowledge, practicality and the well-being of all involved.

What do we cover?

Chapter 1, Understanding the Legal Framework, delves into the Surrogacy Act in Queensland, outlining its key principles, objectives and legal definitions. From eligibility requirements to parental responsibilities, this chapter provides a foundational understanding of the legal landscape surrounding surrogacy arrangements.

Chapter 2: Eligibility Requirements explores the criteria for intended parents, including the importance of establishing a medical or social need for the surrogacy arrangement. Through case studies and practical examples, this chapter explores the fundamental requirements individuals and couples must consider to fulfil their dreams of parenthood.

Chapter 3: Navigating the Surrogacy Process offers a step-by-step guide to the surrogacy journey, from connecting with a surrogate to obtaining a parentage order. By breaking down each stage of the process, this chapter equips you with the knowledge needed to navigate the surrogacy journey effectively.

Chapter 4: The Importance of Open Communication emphasises the significance of transparent and honest communication among all parties involved in the surrogacy process. From building trust with your surrogate to managing expectations and concerns proactively, this chapter highlights the pivotal role of communication in fostering positive relationships and navigating potential challenges.

Chapter 5: Understanding the Costs provides insights into the financial aspects of surrogacy, including budgeting for expenses, exploring financial support options and managing reimbursement arrangements. By addressing the financial considerations upfront, intended parents can approach the surrogacy process with greater clarity and preparedness.

Chapter 6: Seeking Emotional Support underscores the importance of emotional well-being throughout the surrogacy journey. From therapy beyond legal requirements to addressing emotional challenges and stressors, this chapter offers practical strategies for maintaining emotional resilience and support.

Chapter 7: Practical Considerations for the Surrogacy Journey and Beyond offers practical advice and insights for navigating various aspects of the surrogacy journey, including honouring the birth mother, managing the surrogacy journey and considering post-surrogacy considerations. By incorporating these practical tips and considerations, intended parents can navigate the surrogacy process with confidence and grace.

Throughout this book, I am hoping to empower you with the knowledge, resources and support needed to embark on the surrogacy journey with confidence. Whether you are considering surrogacy as an intended parent or contemplating becoming a surrogate, this book is your guide to navigating the legal process of surrogacy in Queensland.

Other things to note about this book

At the time of writing this book, there is no national framework for surrogacy matters. Each State and Territory in Australia has its own law and process and many of the steps are similar. It is important, however, that you seek advice from a lawyer in the State or Territory where you live so that you have advice as it relates to your individual circumstances.

Throughout the chapters of this book, you'll find detailed explanations of **the legal requirements for surrogacy in Queensland**, along with practical tips for each stage of the process. From establishing eligibility and connecting with a surrogate to navigating the legal and emotional aspects of surrogacy, my aim is to provide comprehensive guidance to empower you on your surrogacy journey.

It's essential to understand that the information provided in this book should not be construed as legal advice. Surrogacy laws and regulations may vary and individual circumstances can significantly impact the surrogacy process. Therefore, **I strongly recommend seeking independent legal advice** tailored to your specific situation to ensure compliance with relevant laws and regulations.

It's important to note that while this book provides valuable information about the legal aspects and practical tips of surrogacy, **this book does not offer medical advice or guidance on the IVF process**. Surrogacy is a complex process that involves medical procedures and considerations best addressed by medical professionals. Therefore, you must consult with your general practitioner or fertility specialist to determine if surrogacy is the right path for you, considering your individual circumstances and medical needs.

With those things in mind, I recommend this book to you. I firmly believe that with information and knowledge comes empowerment, allowing you to make the best decisions for you.

I hope this book serves as a valuable resource, offering clarity, support and guidance every step of the way.

Elizabeth

July 2025

Chapter 1:

Understanding the Legal Framework

Understanding the legal aspects of surrogacy is essential for all parties involved, as it forms the foundation for the entire surrogacy journey. This chapter will explore the key legal definitions and terminology relevant to surrogacy in Queensland. We will also examine the responsibilities of all parties involved in the surrogacy process, emphasising the paramount importance of prioritising the well-being and best interests of the child, the basis for all legal decisions in surrogacy in Queensland.

Surrogacy is a deeply personal and emotionally complex journey and navigating its legal landscape can often be challenging. However, by gaining a comprehensive understanding of the legal framework, you can ensure that you start the process with the information you need for a smooth surrogacy journey.

OVERVIEW OF THE SURROGACY ACT IN QUEENSLAND

The Surrogacy Act 2010 (Qld) is the primary legal framework governing surrogacy arrangements in Queensland. The legislation provides a set of rules and guidelines designed to regulate surrogacy, protect the rights of all parties involved and ensure the best interests and well-being of the child born through surrogacy.

At its core, the Surrogacy Act aims to establish clear procedures and requirements for surrogacy arrangements while safeguarding the welfare of the child and addressing the legal complexities inherent in such arrangements. It sets out the responsibilities of intended parents and birth parents (surrogates) and the process for a successful transfer of parentage.

Section 5 sets out the main objects of the Act. They are:

(a) *to* ***regulate particular matters in relation to surrogacy*** *arrangements, including by* ***prohibiting commercial surrogacy*** *arrangements and providing, in particular circumstances, for the* ***court-sanctioned transfer of parentage*** *of a child born as a result of a surrogacy arrangement; and*

(b) *in the context of a surrogacy arrangement that may result in the court-sanctioned transfer of parentage of a child born as a result—*

(i) *to* ***establish procedures to ensure parties to the arrangement understand its nature and implications****; and*

(ii) ***to safeguard the child's well-being and best interests****.*

Section 6 sets out the guiding principles. They are:

(1) *that the* ***well-being and best interests of a child*** *born as a result of a surrogacy arrangement, both through childhood and for the rest of his or her life, are paramount.*

(2) *that—*

(a) *a child born as a result of a surrogacy arrangement should be cared for in a way that—*

(i) *ensures a* ***safe, stable and nurturing family and home life****; and*

(ii) ***promotes openness and honesty about the child's birth parentage****; and*

(iii) *promotes the* ***development of the child's emotional, mental, physical and social well-being****;*

(b) *the* ***same status, protection and support should be available to a child born as a result of a surrogacy arrangement*** *regardless of—*

(i) *how the child was conceived under the arrangement; or*

(i) *whether there is a genetic relationship between the child and any of the parties to the arrangement; or*

(ii) *the relationship status of the persons who become the child's parents as a result of a transfer of parentage;*

(c) *the long-**term health and well-being of parties to a surrogacy arrangement and their families** should be promoted;*

(d) *the **autonomy of consenting adults in their private lives should be respected**.*

Key provisions in the Act include definitions of important terms related to surrogacy, requirements for eligibility to participate in surrogacy arrangements, procedures for obtaining legal parentage of the child and guidelines for the preparation and execution of surrogacy agreements. Additionally, the Act outlines the legal consequences of surrogacy, including the implications for parental rights and obligations, financial arrangements and the role of the court in overseeing surrogacy proceedings.

By providing a clear legal framework, the Act aims to ensure transparency, fairness and the protection of all parties involved, ultimately contributing to the ethical and responsible practice of surrogacy.

KEY LEGAL DEFINITIONS AND TERMINOLOGY

Understanding the key legal definitions and terminology that form the foundation of surrogacy arrangements is crucial. These definitions clarify the roles and responsibilities of the parties involved.

The first important term is "**birth mother**" – you might think of this person colloquially as the "**surrogate**". We use both birth mother and surrogate interchangeably within this book. The birth mother is the woman who carries and gives birth to a child on behalf of the intended parents. Surrogates play a vital role in the surrogacy process, offering their assistance to help others achieve their dream of parenthood. Linked to the "birth mother" is the **birth mother's spouse**. This is the person who is in a relationship with the mother throughout the surrogacy process. Together, they are called the "**birth parents**".

You will find the legal definition of birth mother, birth mother's spouse and birth parents in **Section 8** of the Act.

*The "**birth mother**" is the woman who agrees to the matters mentioned in section 7 (1) (a) under a surrogacy arrangement, that is, the woman agrees to become, or try to become, pregnant with the intention that—*

(i) *a child born as a result of the pregnancy is to be treated as the child, not of the woman, but of the other person or persons; and*

(ii) *the woman will relinquish to the other person or persons custody and guardianship of a child born as a result of the pregnancy*

*The "**birth mother's spouse**" means the birth mother's spouse at the time when the birth mother entered into the surrogacy arrangement.*

*A "**birth parent**" of a child means a person (other than an intended parent) who is recognised at law as being a parent of the child at the time when the child is born.*

"**Intended parents**" refer to the individuals or couples who ask the birth mother to carry a child on their behalf. They are typically individuals who are unable to conceive or carry a child themselves due to medical reasons or other circumstances.

Section 9 sets out the legal definition of intended parent and couple as follows:

*An "**intended parent**" is a person who agrees to the matter mentioned in section 7 (1) (b) under a surrogacy arrangement, that is, the person or persons who agree* *to become permanently responsible for the custody and guardianship of a child born as a result of the pregnancy.*

*A "**couple**" is a person and the person's spouse.*

As a group, the intended parents and the birth parents agree to enter into a written agreement known as the "**surrogacy arrangement**." The surrogacy arrangement outlines the agreement between the parties about the surrogacy process, including the rights and obligations of all parties involved. This document sets out the framework for the surrogacy journey, covering aspects such as medical procedures, financial arrangements and future parental rights.

Section 7 of the Act sets out the meaning of surrogacy arrangement as *an arrangement, agreement or understanding between a woman and another person or persons under which—*

(a) *the woman agrees to become, or try to become, pregnant with the intention that—*

  (i) *a child born as a result of the pregnancy is to be treated as the child, not of the woman, but of the other person or persons; and*

  (ii) *the woman will relinquish to the other person or persons custody and guardianship of a child born as a result of the pregnancy; and*

(b) *the other* person *or persons agree to become permanently responsible for the custody and guardianship of a child born as a result of the pregnancy.*

There may be other parties to a surrogacy arrangement, for example, the woman's spouse.

Also, there may be other matters dealt with in a surrogacy arrangement.

Finally, it is essential to understand that "**commercial surrogacy" is illegal in all States and Territories in Australia**.

You will have seen in the objects of the Act, set out in Section 5, this opening sentence:

to regulate particular matters in relation to surrogacy arrangements, including by ***prohibiting commercial surrogacy arrangements*** *and providing, in particular circumstances, for the court-sanctioned transfer of parentage of a child born as a result of a surrogacy arrangement*

What is commercial surrogacy? **Commercial surrogacy** refers to an arrangement in which a woman (the surrogate) is compensated financially or materially beyond reimbursement of medical and other reasonable expenses for carrying and delivering a child to the intended parents. In commercial surrogacy, money or valuable consideration is exchanged for the services of the birth mother in carrying and delivering a child.

Generally, the birth mother receives payment or a fee for her services in addition to reimbursement for medical and other related expenses. The commercial arrangements are typically formalised through legally binding contracts outlining the rights, responsibilities and expectations of all parties.

There are serious ethical considerations relating to commercial surrogacy, particularly relating to the autonomy of the birth mother, the welfare of the child and the implications that financial incentives have on reproductive arrangements. This is why the legal status of commercial surrogacy varies widely around the world.

In contrast, **altruistic surrogacy**, which is legal in Queensland and many other places, involves no financial gain for the surrogate beyond reimbursement of expenses directly related to the pregnancy and birth. The primary motivation in altruistic surrogacy is typically to assist another person or couple in having a child rather than financial compensation.

Knowing and understanding these key legal definitions and terminology is essential when you are embarking on a surrogacy journey in Queensland. Understanding the role of each party involved, particularly the birth mother and her spouse, contributes to the smooth process of your surrogacy journey.

RIGHTS AND RESPONSIBILITIES OF PARTIES INVOLVED

Using the term "rights" can be difficult in surrogacy. When parties enter a surrogacy arrangement, they agree to a process based entirely on good faith. The reason for this is that you are unable to enter into a written contract and thereafter enforce a contract that requires a person to fall pregnant, carry that pregnancy and, after that, hand over a child at the end of the pregnancy. There is no legal right to enforce that process.

The surrogacy arrangement, at best, is the recording of an in-principle good faith agreement that the parties to the agreement will do what they can to try to make a baby and at the end of the day, the intended parents will be that baby's parents. For those reasons, using words like "rights" is inherently difficult in surrogacy matters.

The birth mother has some rights. She has the right to manage the pregnancy in accordance with her own needs, subject, of course, to any medical advice. The birth mother has a right to be reimbursed for reasonable surrogacy costs (medical and legal costs) incurred throughout the surrogacy process.

The child born as a result of a surrogacy arrangement has inherent rights to be protected, nurtured and cared for in a safe and loving environment. It is the collective responsibility of all parties involved, including the intended parents and the birth parents, to ensure that the child's best interests are prioritised throughout the surrogacy journey.

Those are the only rights that arise out of the surrogacy process.

Each party to a surrogacy arrangement has specific responsibilities to ensure the protection and well-being of everyone involved in the surrogacy journey, with a primary focus on the well-being and best interests of the child.

While not a legal responsibility, intended parents do have the responsibility to provide support, care and financial assistance to the surrogate during the surrogacy process, as well as to the child once born.

Surrogates, or birth mothers, have the responsibility to adhere to the terms of the surrogacy agreement and prioritise the health and well-being of both themselves and the child they are carrying.

Ultimately, remember that the goal of a surrogacy arrangement is to make a baby for a person or couple who desperately wants to have a baby. Understanding that all parties involved have limited legal rights and significant personal responsibilities is essential. Knowing that you are entering into a "good faith" agreement from the start will avoid confusion about whether rights exist in the future.

CONCLUDING THOUGHTS

This chapter has provided an overview of surrogacy arrangements and the key people involved. My three key takeaways from this chapter are:

1. Familiarising yourself with the key legal definitions and terminology used in the Surrogacy Act is essential. Understanding these terms allows you to navigate the legal landscape with confidence.

2. Throughout the surrogacy process, the well-being and best interests of the child must remain paramount. This principle underscores the importance of approaching surrogacy arrangements with a commitment to safeguarding the child's welfare and ensuring their long-term happiness and stability.
3. It is critical to know that there are few rights within a surrogacy context, many personal responsibilities and a lot of good faith. By prioritising open communication, mutual respect and adherence to legal requirements, you can navigate the surrogacy journey in a manner that honours all involved.

What are your key takeaways? Pull out your highlighter and sticky tabs, or make some notes below.

Chapter 2:

Eligibility Requirements

Surrogacy is a deeply personal and complex journey and understanding the criteria for eligibility is crucial when embarking on this path. The Act outlines specific requirements that intended parents must meet to qualify for surrogacy arrangements, ensuring that the process is conducted ethically, legally and in the best interests of all parties involved.

This chapter will explore the eligibility criteria in the Surrogacy Act. We will delve into the definitions of medical and social need outlined in the legislation, highlighting the circumstances under which individuals or couples may be deemed eligible for surrogacy arrangements. By understanding these eligibility requirements, you can make informed decisions about whether surrogacy is the right option for building your family.

CRITERIA FOR INTENDED PARENTS

The Act outlines the eligibility requirements for intended parents seeking to embark on a surrogacy arrangement. This section establishes the criteria for determining whether there exists a medical or social need for the arrangement.

For applications for a parentage order, the presence of a medical or social need for the surrogacy arrangement is crucial. If there is only one intended parent involved, this need is established if the intended parent is either a man or an eligible woman, as defined by the Act. Similarly, if there are two intended parents, the need is present if they are either a man and an eligible woman, two men, or two eligible women.

The Act defines an "**eligible woman**" as a woman who meets specific criteria related to her ability to conceive and carry a pregnancy. This includes situations where the woman is unable to conceive, likely unable to carry a pregnancy or give birth due to medical grounds, or where pregnancy or birth poses significant health risks to her. Additionally, eligibility extends to women likely to conceive a child affected by certain genetic conditions or disorders or whose health is likely to be significantly affected by pregnancy or birth. These criteria underscore the importance of ensuring that surrogacy arrangements are entered into with careful consideration of the medical and social circumstances of the intended parents.

Specifically, **Section 14** notes the definition of eligible woman as follows:

An ***"eligible woman"*** *is a woman who—*

(a) *is unable to conceive; or*

(b) *if able to conceive—*

  (i) *is likely to be unable, on medical grounds, either to carry a pregnancy or to give birth; or*

  (ii) *either—*

    (A) *is* unlikely *to survive a pregnancy or birth; or*

    (B) *is likely to have her health significantly affected by a pregnancy or birth; or*

  (iii) *is likely to conceive—*

    (A) *a child affected by a genetic condition or disorder, the cause of which is attributable to the woman; or*

    (B) *a child who is unlikely to survive a pregnancy or birth; or*

    (C) *a child whose health is likely to be significantly affected by a pregnancy or birth.*

CASE STUDIES

Here are some case studies that highlight the different circumstances in which surrogacy can be an option if you are unable to have children.

Case Study: Colin and Laura

Colin and Laura have been married for three years and are keen to have a child. Laura is unable to carry a child because she has recently recovered from cancer treatment and surgery, which resulted in Laura having her uterus removed. After careful consideration, they decide to pursue surrogacy. Laura meets the criteria of an eligible woman under the Act, where she cannot conceive and carry a pregnancy.

Case Study: Eli and Rachel

Eli and Rachel have been trying to conceive for several years but have faced multiple miscarriages and fertility challenges. After exhausting all other options, they decide to pursue surrogacy. Rachel meets the criteria of an eligible woman where, though she has been able to conceive a child, she is unable, on medical grounds, to carry the pregnancy to full term.

Case Study: Lisa and Emily

Lisa and Emily are a same-sex female couple who have been in a committed relationship for seven years. They had always dreamed of starting a family together. However, when they began to look into their options, it became apparent that Lisa had a rare genetic condition that would affect any child that she was to have in the future. Emily did not have any genetic conditions and the testing indicated that she was likely to conceive and carry a pregnancy successfully. On that basis, Lisa and Emily were not eligible for surrogacy because Emily is not an eligible woman under the Act.

Case Study: David and Kyle

David and Kyle are a same-sex male couple who have been together for ten years. They have always wanted to become parents and after exploring their options, they decide that surrogacy is the best way to fulfil their dreams. As a same-sex male couple, they meet the criteria outlined in the Act, which allows them to pursue surrogacy.

Case Study: Michelle and James

Michelle and James are a heterosexual couple who have been married for five years. They have always dreamed of having a family together. Michelle has been diagnosed with severe anxiety and depression, which makes it difficult for her to conceive and carry a pregnancy. Carrying a baby would likely significantly impact her health. Michelle's anxiety will cause stress to her body which is likely to impact her ability to carry a child. Due to Michelle's psychological condition, their fertility specialist recommends surrogacy as the safest option for starting a family. They understand that while Michelle may be physically capable of conceiving, her mental health would be significantly impacted by the stress and emotional toll of pregnancy. Therefore, surrogacy is seen as the most suitable and least risky path to parenthood for them.

CONCLUDING THOUGHTS

It is essential to understand the eligibility requirements for surrogacy arrangements. It is likely that if you are looking at surrogacy as an option, you have will understood the medical requirements and discussed those with your medical team. There are strict eligibility requirements and surrogacy is not an option open to everyone.

My key takeaways are these:

1. Eligibility for surrogacy is based on medical or social need, emphasising the importance of demonstrating a genuine necessity for the surrogacy arrangement. Whether facing infertility challenges, medical conditions preventing pregnancy, or other significant obstacles to conception, you must carefully assess your circumstances to determine if you meet the criteria outlined in the legislation.
2. Each surrogacy journey is unique and eligibility requirements must be assessed on a case-by-case basis.
3. Whether pursuing surrogacy as a heterosexual couple, a same-sex couple, or an individual, prospective you should seek personalised guidance to navigate the complexities of eligibility determination. By consulting with medical experts and surrogacy counsellors, you can gain clarity on your eligibility status and make informed decisions about your path forward.

What are your key takeaways? Pull out your highlighter and sticky tabs, or make some notes below.

Chapter 3:

Navigating the Surrogacy Process

Embarking on a surrogacy journey can be both exciting and overwhelming, filled with anticipation and hope for the future. This chapter breaks down the intricacies of the surrogacy process into ten essential steps. From establishing the initial need for surrogacy to the final court decision granting the parentage order, each stage plays a crucial role in realising the dream of parenthood through surrogacy.

We will explore each step in detail, providing insights and guidance to help you navigate the complexities of the surrogacy process with confidence and clarity. By understanding the significance of each milestone and the tasks involved, you can approach the process with informed decision-making and proactive engagement.

THE SURROGACY PROCESS

The surrogacy journey weaves its way through legal, emotional and medical processes, all of them critical to ensuring a successful pregnancy and transfer of parentage. The ten key steps in the surrogacy process are:

1. Establishing a Medical or Social Need
2. Connecting with a Surrogate
3. Assessing Medical Requirements: Ensuring Compatibility
4. The Importance of Counselling
5. Recording your Surrogacy Agreement and Getting Legal Advice
6. Embracing Milestones: Conception, Pregnancy and Birth
7. Registering the Birth
8. Further Counselling and Surrogacy Guidance Reports
9. Applying for a Parentage Order
10. Court Decision to Grant the Parentage Order

Let's work our way through each step.

STEP 1: ESTABLISHING A MEDICAL OR SOCIAL NEED

The first step in the surrogacy journey is to establish whether you are eligible. In Chapter 2, we reviewed the eligibility requirements to establish a medical or social need for surrogacy.

Practically, to begin this process, you will meet with your general practitioner to discuss your fertility struggles and explore potential avenues for parenthood. Upon evaluation, your general practitioner may refer you to a fertility specialist who can provide further insight and guidance.

The fertility specialist plays a pivotal role in assessing the medical requirements and determining the suitability for surrogacy. After undergoing attempts at IVF treatment and other fertility interventions without success, surrogacy may emerge as a recommended path forward.

By working closely with your fertility specialist you can establish whether a medical or social need exists and explore the next steps toward creating your family.

STEP 2: CONNECTING WITH A SURROGATE

Once you have established a medical or social need for surrogacy, one of the most personal steps in the surrogacy process is connecting with a surrogate. For some, this may involve turning to family or friends who generously offer to assist in this incredible journey. However, for others, finding a surrogate means reaching out to someone they have not yet met.

Your family and close friends may or may not be aware of your fertility struggles, particularly where couples may consider this to be a private part of their relationship. Others may be open about their pregnancy attempts. Wherever you fall in this dynamic, be open and honest in your communication with family and friends and respectful of any responses you receive. Remember, it is a significant undertaking for the birth mother, both medically and emotionally and she and her partner may just not be up for it.

For those tasked with finding an independent birth mother, intended parents often join surrogacy forums and support groups, where they can seek advice, share experiences and connect with potential surrogates. These communities provide invaluable support and guidance, offering support and understanding amidst the complexities of the surrogacy journey. In addition to online resources, fertility clinics can also be instrumental in facilitating connections between intended parents and surrogates.

Once a connection is established, nurturing and fostering the relationship with the surrogate is essential. Building trust, open communication and mutual respect are the cornerstones of a successful surrogacy journey. Intended parents should take the time to meet with and get to know their birth mother, fostering a sense of partnership and shared commitment to the remarkable journey ahead.

STEP 3: ASSESSING MEDICAL REQUIREMENTS: ENSURING COMPATIBILITY

The third step is to ensure that the birth mother is medically compatible. In agreeing to be the birth mother, your surrogate will need to meet with medical specialists, ensure that she can carry your child and complete all medical tests and procedures that are required. It can be an invasive process, which is why it is important to ensure that the relationship with your birth mother (whether they are family, friends or a new connection) starts with a solid foundation.

If your medical team approves the connection, then, subject to your counselling and legal requirements, you are ready to move forward.

STEP 4: THE IMPORTANCE OF COUNSELLING

As well as being a mandated legal requirement, counselling plays a crucial role in the surrogacy process. An appropriately qualified counsellor must be engaged to prepare a report recommending the surrogacy arrangement **before it proceeds**. This report is a vital component in the surrogacy journey, offering insights and recommendations that contribute to informed decision-making and safeguard the well-being of all parties involved.

Beyond fulfilling legal obligations, counselling offers other benefits to both birth parents and intended parents. For birth parents, counselling provides a supportive space to explore their motivations, expectations and concerns surrounding the surrogacy process. It can help them navigate complex emotions, such as grief, loss and the challenges of relinquishing parental rights.

Similarly, intended parents can benefit significantly from counselling as they navigate the process of surrogacy. Counselling sessions offer a platform to discuss hopes, fears and practical considerations related to the surrogacy journey. It provides an opportunity to clarify expectations, establish boundaries and strengthen communication with the surrogate, fostering a sense of trust and mutual respect. Additionally, counselling equips intended parents with coping strategies and resilience-building techniques to navigate the inevitable ups and downs of the surrogacy process with resilience and grace.

Here are some definitions to consider. **Section 19** of the Act notes that an "**appropriately qualified**" **counsellor** is either a member of the Australian and New Zealand Infertility Counsellors Association, a psychiatrist, a psychologist or a social worker who has the experience, skills or knowledge to prepare a report. This counsellor will later prepare an affidavit as part of the Application for a Parentage Order to confirm they met with all parties and completed counselling about the surrogacy arrangement and its social and psychological implications **before** the surrogacy arrangement was made.

STEP 5: RECORDING YOUR SURROGACY AGREEMENT AND SEEKING LEGAL ADVICE

The next step in the surrogacy journey is recording your surrogacy agreement in writing and obtaining legal advice. This step is not only essential for legal compliance but also lays the groundwork for a clear understanding of rights, responsibilities and expectations for all parties involved. **Before conception occurs**, it is a legal requirement in Queensland for both the intended parents and the birth parents to receive legal advice about the surrogacy process and to enter into a written surrogacy agreement.

The surrogacy agreement serves as a foundational document that outlines the intentions of the surrogacy arrangement. It covers various aspects such as the agreement to the surrogacy process, an intention to work together to create a viable pregnancy, how the pregnancy is to be managed, the arrangements after birth and the intention to seek a parentage order. A comprehensive surrogacy agreement helps mitigate potential conflicts and uncertainties down the road, providing a framework for a harmonious and well-defined surrogacy journey.

Seeking legal advice from a qualified surrogacy lawyer is crucial to ensure that the surrogacy agreement complies with legal requirements and adequately protects the interests of both birth parents and intended parents. Legal advice offers invaluable insights into the legal implications, rights and responsibilities associated with surrogacy, empowering parties to make informed decisions and navigate potential challenges confidently.

Pause here to remember my comments in Chapter 1 about the "rights" and responsibilities of parties to a surrogacy arrangement and the overall understanding that in "good faith", parties agree to bring a child into the world without any legal obligation to do so.

In particular, **Section 15** states that **a surrogacy arrangement is not enforceable**.

Section 15 goes on to say that an obligation to pay or reimburse the birth mother's costs is only enforceable unless the birth mother refuses to relinquish custody of the child or does not consent to the making of the parentage order.

A lawyer must provide advice about the following:

(i) *the unenforceable nature of the arrangement, other than as provided under section 15*

(ii) *the person's legal obligations under the arrangement and this Act*

(iii) *the legal implications if the birth mother does not relinquish the child, including whether child support would be payable by the child's biological father under the Child Support (Assessment) Act 1989 (Cwlth)*

(iv) *the legal implications if, after the birth of the child, the intended parents do not want to be permanently responsible for the child's custody and guardianship*

(v) *the legal implications if, after the birth of the child, the birth mother, the birth mother's spouse (if any), another birth parent (if any) and the intended parents do not want to be permanently responsible for the child's custody and guardianship*

(vi) *the legal implications of the making of a parentage order*

(vii) *that this Act promotes openness and honesty about the child's birth parentage*

At the end of the surrogacy process, the lawyer must provide an affidavit confirming that independent advice was provided to either the birth parents or the intended parents and that their client appeared to understand the advice provided. Those details are set out in Section 30 of the Act.

The IVF process is unable to commence without a counselling report and a written surrogacy arrangement. The written surrogacy arrangement cannot be finalised without legal advice.

STEP 6: EMBRACING MILESTONES: CONCEPTION, PREGNANCY AND BIRTH

After navigating through the essential steps of counselling, legal requirements and paperwork, the surrogacy journey progresses to one of its most pivotal phases: embracing the milestones of conception, pregnancy and birth. With the groundwork laid and agreements in place, both the intended parents and the birth parents can embark on the remarkable journey of bringing a new life into the world.

Conception marks the beginning of this chapter, as assisted reproductive technologies such as in vitro fertilisation (IVF) are employed to facilitate the fertilisation of eggs and the creation of embryos. For intended parents, this stage may involve emotional highs and lows as they navigate the intricacies of fertility treatments and eagerly await news of successful conception. Meanwhile, the birth mother plays a crucial role in this process, offering her selfless dedication and support to help fulfil the dreams of others.

As the journey progresses, the **pregnancy** becomes a shared experience filled with anticipation, joy and perhaps some challenges along the way. From attending prenatal appointments to witnessing the miraculous milestones of fetal development, both the intended parents and the surrogate are united in their commitment to nurturing and supporting the growing life within. It is a time marked by bonding, empathy and mutual respect as they navigate the highs and lows of the pregnancy journey together.

Finally, the long-awaited moment arrives with **the birth of the child**, marking the culmination of months of anticipation, preparation and unwavering dedication. Whether through natural birth or caesarean delivery, the baby's arrival is a transformative experience for all involved, symbolising the fulfilment of dreams, hopes and aspirations. In this moment of joy and celebration, the bonds forged between the intended parents and the surrogate are forever cemented, creating a legacy of love, gratitude and shared humanity that transcends biology and genetics.

STEP 7: REGISTERING THE BIRTH

Once the miracle of birth has occurred and the child enters the world, the next crucial step in the surrogacy journey is registering the birth. This process involves completing an application to register the birth, which carries significant legal and practical implications for all parties involved. The birth parents – comprising the birth mother and her partner, if applicable – are recognised as the legal parents of the child upon birth.

The registration process requires careful attention to detail, ensuring that all required information is accurately provided and the necessary documentation is submitted promptly. While the intended parents typically play an active role in this process, the birth parents must formally register the birth and attest to the accuracy of the information provided.

One key aspect of registering the birth is selecting the child's name, including their surname – a decision typically made by the intended parents. This symbolic act holds deep significance, as it marks the child's formal entry into the family unit and reflects the hopes, dreams and identity of their newfound kinship.

It is imperative that the original birth certificate accurately reflects the identities of the birth parents, including both the birth mother and her partner. Failure to do so may lead to complications later in the surrogacy process, particularly during the subsequent application for a parentage order. Therefore, attention to detail and the legal requirements are essential at this stage, laying the foundation for a seamless transition towards securing legal recognition of parentage for the intended parents.

STEP 8: FURTHER COUNSELLING AND SURROGACY GUIDANCE REPORT

The surrogacy journey is not just a legal and medical process – it is also a personal and emotional experience that requires ongoing support and guidance. As part of this holistic approach, all parties involved in the surrogacy arrangement are required to undergo further counselling with an independent appropriately qualified counsellor. These additional counselling sessions serve multiple purposes, including ensuring that everyone fully comprehends the social and psychological implications of seeking a parentage order.

During these counselling sessions, which are separate from the initial counselling required earlier in the process, the counsellor engages with the birth mother, her spouse and the intended parents. Through these interactions, the counsellor gains insight into each party's perspective, concerns and hopes regarding the surrogacy journey. The goal is to foster open and honest communication among all parties, promoting a shared understanding of the challenges and opportunities that lie ahead.

Following the counselling sessions, the counsellor prepares a comprehensive Surrogacy Guidance Report, which captures the key insights and recommendations from the interviews. This report plays a pivotal role in the parentage order application process, providing the court with information regarding the emotional and psychological dynamics of the surrogacy arrangement. Ultimately, the report aims to assess whether the proposed parentage order aligns with the best interests and well-being of the child, emphasising the importance of transparency, stability and nurturing family relationships in shaping the child's future.

Section 32 of the Act notes that an independent and appropriately qualified counsellor must prepare a **surrogacy guidance report**. Aside from their qualifications, the report confirms that the counsellor met with all parties and notes the date or dates of any appointments. Importantly, the counsellor must form a view about each person's understanding of:

(a) *the social and psychological implications of the making of a parentage order on the child and relevant persons.*

(b) *openness and honesty about the child's birth parentage being for the well-being and in the best interests, of the child.*

The report must also set out the care arrangements that the applicant, or joint applicants, have proposed for the child and whether making a parentage order would be for the well-being and in the child's best interests.

STEP 9: APPLYING FOR A PARENTAGE ORDER

The next and most critical step in the surrogacy journey is applying for a parentage order. This legal process transfers parental rights from the birth parents to the intended parents. This process is subject to strict criteria outlined in the Act, which the court must thoroughly assess before granting the order.

First and foremost, the court must be satisfied that **granting the parentage order would be in the best interests and well-being of the child**. This consideration underscores the paramount importance of prioritising the child's welfare throughout the surrogacy process. Additionally, the child must have lived with the intended parents for at least 28 consecutive days before the application is made, reinforcing the establishment of a stable and nurturing family environment.

The application must comply with various legal and procedural requirements, including evidence of a medical or social need for the surrogacy arrangement and confirmation that all parties involved obtained independent legal advice and counselling before entering the surrogacy agreement. The court also requires explicit consent from the birth mother and her spouse and intended parents, along with a supportive surrogacy guidance report that reinforces the appropriateness of granting the parentage order. These criteria ensure that the surrogacy process is conducted ethically, transparently and with the child's best interests at heart.

In particular, **section 21** sets out the requirements for an application for a parentage order.

The application must be made not less than 28 days and not more than six months after the child's birth or at a later time with the court's leave. For the Court to grant a late application, it must be satisfied that there are exceptional circumstances and that it is for the well-being and in the best interests of the child to grant leave.

Section 22 outlines the information the Court must consider when making a parentage order. The court may make the parentage order only if it is satisfied of all of the following matters:

(a) *the proposed order will be for the well-being and in the best interests, of the child.*

(b) *the child has lived with the applicant for at least 28 days before the application is made, was living with the applicants at the time the application was made and is living with applicants at the time of the hearing.*

(c) *the applicant, or joint applicants, were entitled to apply under section 21.*

(d) *there is evidence of a medical or social need for the surrogacy arrangement.*

(e) *the surrogacy arrangement was made after the parties each obtained independent legal advice and was made after each party obtained counselling from an appropriately qualified counsellor about the surrogacy arrangements and its social and psychological implications. The arrangement must also have been by consent of all parties, made before the child was conceived and is in writing and signed by the parties..*

(f) *the birth mother and the birth mother's spouse (if any) were at least 25 years when the surrogacy arrangement was made.*

(g) *the applicant, or each of the joint applicants, was at least 25 years old when the surrogacy arrangement was made and resident in Queensland.*

(h) *the birth mother, the birth mother's spouse (if any), another birth parent (if any) and the applicant, or joint applicants, consent to the making of the parentage order at the time of the hearing.*

(i) *a surrogacy guidance report under section 32 supports the making of the proposed order.*

The Court can dispense with some requirements in Section 22; however, others are mandatory. Those exceptions are in Section 23. The court must be satisfied that there are exceptional circumstances to dispense with the usual requirements.

Required Documents for Court Application

Section 25 of the Act sets out the documents required when applying for a parentage order. These documents are crucial in facilitating the legal process and ensuring compliance with legislative requirements.

First and foremost, a copy of the child's birth certificate must be provided, serving as foundational documentation for the application. Additionally, a copy of the surrogacy arrangement outlining the terms and agreements between the parties involved is essential for the court's review.

Affidavits from the applicant or joint applicants, the birth mother and any other birth parent involved in the arrangement are required, as are affidavits from legal advisors and appropriately qualified counsellors. This ensures that all parties have received adequate guidance and support. Finally, affidavits from medical practitioners corroborate the medical necessity or eligibility of the applicants, especially in cases where an eligible woman is involved.

Together, these documents provide comprehensive evidence for the court that outlines the legal and medical intricacies of the surrogacy arrangement and serves as a testament to the careful consideration and due diligence exercised throughout the process.

Section 25 outlines the documents and information to be produced to the Court. Each affidavit must comply with its own section of the Act. The documents are:

(a) *a copy of the child's birth certificate.*

(b) *a copy of the surrogacy arrangement.*

(c) *an affidavit under section 26 sworn by the applicant, or joint applicants.*

(d) *an affidavit under section 27 sworn by the birth mother.*

(e) *an affidavit under section 28 sworn by the birth mother's spouse (if any).*

(f) *an affidavit under section 29 sworn by another birth parent (if any).*

(g) *for the applicant, or each joint applicant, the birth mother and the birth mother's spouse (if any) – an affidavit under section 30 sworn by the lawyer who gave legal advice to the person before the surrogacy arrangement was made.*

(h) *an affidavit under section 31 sworn by the appropriately qualified counsellor who gave counselling to the birth mother, the birth mother's spouse (if any) and the applicant, or each joint applicant, before the surrogacy arrangement was made.*

(i) *an affidavit sworn by the independent and appropriately qualified counsellor who, for the purpose of the application, interviewed the birth mother, the birth mother's spouse (if any), another birth parent (if any) and the applicant, or joint applicants; and verifying a surrogacy guidance report under section 32 prepared by the counsellor.*

(j) *for each applicant who is a woman, an affidavit from an appropriately qualified medical practitioner verifying a report prepared by the medical practitioner as to why the applicant is an eligible woman.*

The sections referred to above set out the specific details that must appear in each of the specific affidavits.

STEP 10: COURT DECISION TO GRANT THE PARENTAGE ORDER

Once the court has reviewed and assessed all the information presented, including the required documents and affidavits and is satisfied with the compliance and fulfilment of legal requirements, the court will make the parentage order.

The issue of the parentage order represents a pivotal moment for all parties involved, affirming the legal rights and responsibilities of the intended parents while providing certainty regarding the child's parentage. Ultimately, the granting of the parentage order symbolises the culmination of a collaborative effort between the parties, courts, legal representatives, medical professionals and all other parties involved, working in unison to ensure the successful realisation of the surrogacy arrangement while upholding the paramount importance of the child's well-being and best interests.

Changing the birth certificate

Once the court has granted the parentage order, the next step for the intended parents is to register the order with the appropriate government authority, typically Births, Deaths and Marriages. This formal registration process ensures that the legal status of the child accurately reflects the parentage established through the surrogacy arrangement.

The outcome of registering the parentage order is the amendment of the child's birth certificate. Upon registration, the birth certificate undergoes necessary revisions to reflect the intended parents as the child's legal parents. This updated documentation accurately captures the child's familial lineage, ensuring clarity regarding parental rights and obligations.

By effecting these legal changes, the intended parents cement their parental status, providing the child with the legal recognition and security necessary for their upbringing and future well-being.

CONCLUDING THOUGHTS

This extensive chapter covers the ten stages of the surrogacy process, a multifaceted journey filled with emotional, legal and practical considerations.

My three key takeaways are these:

1. Communication and transparency are paramount. Building strong, open relationships with your surrogate, healthcare providers, legal counsel and support network is essential for navigating the complexities of the surrogacy process effectively.
2. Complying with legal requirements is non-negotiable. From obtaining legal advice and counselling to drafting comprehensive surrogacy agreements and fulfilling court requirements, compliance with legal procedures ensures a smooth and legally sound surrogacy journey.
3. Patience and resilience are virtues to cherish. The surrogacy process often involves unforeseen challenges and emotional highs and lows. By maintaining a positive outlook, seeking support when needed and staying committed to the end goal, you can navigate the surrogacy process with confidence and perseverance.

What are your key takeaways? Pull out your highlighter and sticky tabs, or make some notes below.

Chapter 4:

Communicate Well

Good communication is the cornerstone of any successful surrogacy journey, fostering trust and mutual respect among all parties involved – intended parents, birth parents and their respective support networks. Where surrogacy involves sensitive decisions, emotional investments and legal outcomes, all of which are intertwined, effective communication becomes even more critical.

This chapter focuses on the importance of communicating well, highlighting how effective communication is essential for understanding and collaboration. Clear communication is the foundation for building solid relationships, addressing concerns and navigating potential challenges.

The Act's primary purpose is to **promote openness and honesty in all aspects of the surrogacy arrangement**. Communicating well, therefore, not only fulfils legal requirements but also cultivates an environment of mutual trust and respect, essential for the well-being of everyone involved.

From the initial stages of establishing a surrogacy agreement to the post-birth transition of parental responsibilities, every step of the journey hinges on effective communication. By fostering an open environment where everyone feels empowered to express their thoughts, feelings and needs, surrogacy arrangements can thrive, nurturing strong bonds and fostering a sense of shared purpose and commitment.

This chapter explores the benefits of good communication, practical considerations and managing expectations, providing practical strategies and insights that facilitate effective communication throughout the surrogacy journey.

THE BENEFITS OF COMMUNICATING WELL

Open communication is fundamental to ensuring the success of your surrogacy arrangement. The Act clearly states that transparency and honesty in all interactions between the involved parties are fundamental. This principle underscores the essence of surrogacy as a collaborative journey built on trust, respect and shared understanding.

Clear and open communication sets the foundation for **establishing realistic expectations and boundaries**. From the outset of the surrogacy process, intended parents and surrogates benefit immensely from candid discussions about their motivations, hopes, concerns and any logistical details. This clarity helps align everyone's understanding of roles, responsibilities and the overall journey ahead, minimising misunderstandings and potential conflicts.

All parties need to feel heard, validated and supported throughout the surrogacy process. Intended parents may experience a range of emotions, from excitement and gratitude to anxiety and uncertainty. Birth parents, too, navigate their own emotional journey, balancing their commitment to helping others with their personal lives and well-being. Regular communication allows for the expression of these feelings in a safe environment, fostering empathy and strengthening the bond between intended parents and surrogates.

Effective communication is also **essential for navigating the practical aspects of surrogacy**, including medical procedures, legal requirements and financial arrangements. Clear communication ensures that all parties are well-informed about medical updates, legal responsibilities and any potential changes or challenges that may arise during the journey. This transparency promotes proactive problem-solving and ensures that decisions are made collaboratively and with everyone's best interests in mind.

Good communication extends beyond the immediate participants in the surrogacy arrangement to include healthcare professionals, legal advisors and support networks. **Coordinating stakeholders** requires clear and timely communication to ensure seamless coordination of care, adherence to legal protocols and access to necessary resources throughout the surrogacy process.

Ultimately, fostering good communication in surrogacy not only enhances the efficiency and smoothness of the journey but also cultivates an environment of trust, respect and empathy among all involved parties. By prioritising open dialogue and actively listening to each other's perspectives you can navigate the complexities of surrogacy with greater confidence and support. This approach not only enhances the likelihood of a positive outcome but also lays the groundwork for enduring relationships built on understanding and shared purpose.

Practical Considerations for Communication

Effective communication is not just about exchanging information but ensuring everyone is on the same page and all views are considered and respected. To communicate well throughout the journey and prevent breakdowns, consider the following practical steps and strategies.

Establishing clear channels of communication from the outset is crucial. This includes working out preferred methods of communication – whether it's face-to-face meetings, phone calls, video chats, or messaging platforms. Agreeing on communication frequency and setting expectations early on helps to maintain regular updates and discussions without ambiguity.

Maintaining open and honest dialogue requires active listening and empathy. Both intended parents and birth parents should feel encouraged to express their thoughts, concerns and emotions without fear of judgment. Practicing reflective listening, where each party summarises and validates the other's perspective, fosters mutual understanding and strengthens the relationship.

Setting boundaries is another vital aspect of practical communication. Respect for personal space and time ensures that discussions remain constructive and focused. Clear boundaries can prevent misunderstandings and mitigate potential conflicts by establishing guidelines for when and how communication should occur, respecting each other's privacy and commitments outside of the surrogacy journey.

Addressing problems promptly and constructively is essential to prevent communication breakdowns. When conflicts or misunderstandings arise, parties should approach discussions calmly and objectively. Using "I" statements to express feelings and concerns, rather than placing blame, encourages a solution-oriented approach. Actively trying to work things out and compromising when necessary demonstrates a commitment to maintaining a positive and supportive communication environment.

Regular check-ins and scheduled meetings can help proactively address any emerging issues or changes in circumstances. These sessions provide opportunities to reassess goals, clarify expectations and adjust plans accordingly. Open communication about progress, concerns and potential challenges ensures that everyone remains informed and involved throughout the surrogacy journey.

Lastly, **leveraging support networks and professional guidance** can enhance communication effectiveness. Involving counsellors, mediators, or surrogacy professionals can provide objective perspectives and facilitate difficult conversations when emotions run high or when navigating complex legal or medical decisions. These professionals can offer valuable insights and strategies for resolving communication challenges, ensuring that the focus remains on the well-being of all parties involved.

These practical suggestions need to be balanced, firstly with your individual circumstances, including the personalities of your surrogacy group and secondly with the need to ensure the process isn't overwhelming. **There is a fine line between micromanaging all parties and the perfect schedule. Sometimes you may need to just go with the flow.**

When you do find the right communications balance, though, you will give all parties the best opportunity to navigate a smoother and more fulfilling surrogacy journey.

MANAGING EXPECTATIONS AND ADDRESSING CONCERNS PROACTIVELY

Managing expectations is crucial in any complex process, where multiple parties are involved with varying emotional, legal and practical considerations. When expectations are not managed well, several challenges and consequences can arise, affecting the overall experience and outcomes for everyone involved.

Unrealistic expectations can lead to disappointment and frustration. Intended parents, for instance, might have idealised visions of the surrogacy journey, expecting everything to proceed smoothly without setbacks. When unexpected challenges arise, such as failed attempts at conception, medical complications, or legal hurdles, unmanaged expectations can intensify stress and emotional strain.

Relationships can be strained if expectations are not managed well. For example, if the birth mother experiences complications during pregnancy or has differing views on medical decisions, conflicts may arise if expectations about roles, responsibilities, or outcomes were not clearly defined or communicated. This strain can impact trust and cooperation, crucial elements for a successful surrogacy arrangement.

Financial expectations also need careful management. Surrogacy involves significant costs, including medical expenses, legal fees, compensation for the surrogate's expenses and other related costs. When you underestimate these financial implications or fail to plan adequately, it can lead to **financial stress and uncertainty**, potentially impacting your ability to support your surrogate and manage unexpected expenses that may arise.

Legal expectations are another critical aspect. Each jurisdiction has specific laws governing surrogacy, including requirements for parentage orders, consent documents and legal responsibilities. Failure to understand or comply with these legal expectations could lead to delays in the surrogacy process, legal disputes, or even the inability to secure legal parentage, which can have long-term implications for all parties involved.

Emotional expectations are equally important. **Both intended parents and birth parents may have emotional expectations about the bond they will develop during the journey, the feelings they will experience at different stages and their roles post-birth**. If these emotional expectations are not aligned can lead to feelings of disappointment, guilt, or resentment if the reality does not match their initial hopes or assumptions.

For those reasons, clear and open communication is essential from the outset. Setting realistic goals and discussing potential challenges openly helps all parties understand the complexities involved in surrogacy. It allows for informed decision-making, proactive planning for contingencies and fostering a supportive environment where everyone feels respected and understood.

Ultimately, managing expectations ensures that all parties are prepared for the realities of the journey, mitigating potential conflicts, reducing stress and enhancing the overall experience of creating a family through surrogacy.

CONCLUDING THOUGHTS

Open communication is the cornerstone of a successful surrogacy arrangement.

My three key takeaways are these:

1. Building trust and rapport between all parties is essential for fostering a supportive and collaborative relationship. Open communication allows you to establish mutual understanding, respect boundaries and navigate challenges with empathy and compassion.
2. Addressing concerns and managing expectations proactively is crucial for ensuring a positive surrogacy experience. Honest and transparent communication allows all parties to voice their thoughts, express their needs and work together to find solutions that meet everyone's needs.
3. Embracing openness and honesty is not simply a goal or ideal but also a legal requirement under the Surrogacy Act. By prioritising clear communication, you can navigate the surrogacy process with integrity and ensure the well-being of all involved.

What are your key takeaways? Pull out your highlighter and sticky tabs, or make some notes below.

Chapter 5:

Understanding the Costs

As you navigate the path to surrogacy, you will be met with various financial considerations that can impact your decision-making and overall experience. From medical expenses and counselling to legal fees, the financial aspect of surrogacy requires careful planning and consideration.

Throughout this chapter, we'll explore the costs associated with surrogacy and provide practical insights into budgeting, managing expenses and exploring financial support options.

By understanding the financial landscape of surrogacy and leveraging available resources, you can embark on your surrogacy journey with greater confidence and peace of mind, knowing that you have the tools and support to navigate the financial aspect of this transformative experience.

BREAKING DOWN THE FINANCIAL COSTS IN SURROGACY

It's essential to be prepared for the financial commitments of surrogacy. Here are some key types of costs you can expect to encounter.

The most significant cost associated with surrogacy involves covering the **medical expenses** incurred throughout the process. This includes fertility treatments, IVF procedures, prenatal care for your birth mother, maternity care and any medical interventions necessary during the pregnancy and birth.

Engaging lawyers is a crucial step in the surrogacy process to ensure compliance with the Surrogacy Act and protect the rights of all parties involved. **Legal fees** may encompass drafting and reviewing surrogacy agreements, obtaining independent legal advice and preparing documentation for parentage orders.

Counselling plays a vital role in surrogacy, helping all parties navigate the emotional, psychological and practical aspects of their roles. Intended parents may need to cover the costs of **counselling sessions** for themselves and the birth parents.

Intended parents are typically responsible for covering any **out-of-pocket expenses for the birth mother related to the surrogacy journey**. These may include lost wages, travel expenses, maternity clothing and other incidentals to support the surrogate's well-being during pregnancy. They also include the expenses relating to the surrogate receiving counselling and independent legal advice.

Section 11 of the Act is relevant here, setting out the meaning of the "**birth mother's surrogacy costs**". Those include any reasonable cost associated with the following:

(a) *becoming or trying to become pregnant*

(b) *a pregnancy or birth*

(c) *the birth mother and her spouse being a party to the surrogacy arrangement or proceedings for a parentage order.*

Further examples are given, which include:

(a) *a reasonable medical cost for the birth mother. A "**medical cost**" means a medical cost to the extent that it is not recoverable under Medicare or any health insurance or other scheme.*

(b) *a reasonable medical cost for the child.*

(c) *a premium payable for health, disability or life insurance that would not have been payable but for the arrangement.*

(d) *a reasonable cost of counselling associated with both the pre-surrogacy counselling and obtaining the surrogacy guidance report.*

(e) *a reasonable legal cost for the birth parents relating to the surrogacy arrangement and the transfer of parentage. A "**legal cost**" includes fees for obtaining legal advice and legal representation, court fees and registry fees associated with registration of a birth and transfer of parentage.*

(f) *the value of the birth mother's lost earnings for leave taken for not more than two months during the birth period or for any other period when the birth mother was unable to work on medical grounds.*

(g) *any other reasonable costs associated with the surrogacy arrangement or the making of the order transferring parentage.*

The Act gives examples for (g), which include travel and accommodation costs for a birth mother who lives interstate and travels to Queensland to undertake a fertility treatment, to consult with an obstetrician or to give birth or travel and accommodation costs associated with a birth mother's attendance at a court hearing about an application for a parentage order if the birth mother does not live near the court.

Though not a common process in Australia, engaging **surrogacy agencies or facilitators** may incur administrative fees for coordinating the process, matching intended parents with surrogates, providing support services and facilitating communication between parties.

Understanding these financial considerations upfront can help you plan effectively and ensure you are prepared for the financial commitments associated with surrogacy. By budgeting for these costs and being clear on expectations early in the process, you can navigate the surrogacy journey with greater confidence and peace of mind.

BUDGETING FOR SURROGACY COSTS

Effective financial planning is crucial when you embark on the surrogacy journey and understanding how to manage expenses responsibly can alleviate stress and ensure a smoother process.

Before diving into the surrogacy process, **creating a comprehensive budget outlining all potential expenses is essential**. This includes medical procedures, legal fees, surrogate expenses, counselling costs and other related expenses. By estimating these costs upfront, you can develop a realistic financial plan and avoid unexpected financial strain along the way.

When it comes to **covering the birth mother's expenses**, you can provide reimbursements for specific costs incurred or offer financial support through alternative means, such as providing a debit or credit card for the surrogate's use. Each approach has its pros and cons and the decision may depend on the preferences of both parties involved. Be clear about the financial arrangements so that everyone is on the same page to avoid disputes.

To manage surrogacy expenses effectively, you can implement several **practical strategies**. These may include setting aside a dedicated savings fund for surrogacy, exploring financing options such as personal loans or fertility financing programs and seeking out cost-saving opportunities where possible. Additionally, maintaining open communication with the surrogate and other parties involved can help identify areas where costs can be minimised without compromising the quality of care and support provided.

Here are some **practical ways you can work together to create a budget**. The aim is to balance managing the finances without the process becoming an all-consuming process where parties feel like they are being monitored or controlled.

1. Establishing **open communication** from the outset is crucial. Both parties should discuss their financial expectations, concerns and limitations. This includes being transparent about their financial capacity to cover medical expenses, legal fees and the surrogate's reimbursement costs.
2. **If one party excels at managing finances**, they can take the lead in creating a detailed budget plan. This might involve outlining projected expenses, setting aside contingency funds and ensuring all financial aspects are covered comprehensively.
3. Define **clear boundaries around financial responsibilities and reimbursements**. Ensure all parties understand what expenses are covered by the intended parents and which ones are eligible for reimbursement to the birth parents. This clarity helps avoid misunderstandings and conflicts later on.
4. Schedule regular meetings to **review the budget together** (without overdoing it). This allows parties to track expenses, adjust financial plans as needed and ensure that funds are being managed responsibly and transparently. It may be that your budget requires adjustment once the realities of day-to-day pregnancy kick in.
5. Understand that unexpected expenses or changes in circumstances may arise during the surrogacy journey. All parties should **be flexible and prepared to adjust the budget when necessary** while maintaining financial stability and meeting their obligations.

Case Study: John, Sarah and Emma

Meet John and Sarah, our intended parent couple, who have been matched with Emma, their surrogate, through an online forum. John, who works in finance, takes the lead in creating a surrogacy budget. He starts by listing all anticipated expenses, including fertility treatments, medical consultations, legal fees and living expenses for Emma during pregnancy.

During their initial budget meeting with Emma, John and Sarah discussed their financial capabilities and agreed to a monthly budget for surrogacy-related expenses. They also discussed their decision to set aside additional funds as a contingency for unexpected medical or legal costs.

While Emma appreciates John's proactive approach to budgeting, she prefers to manage her day-to-day expenses independently. Emma, John and Sarah discuss how they can make this work. They agree that John and Sarah will set up an account with a debit card that Emma can use as she requires for agreed expenses. If other eligible expenses related to her pregnancy arise, Emma, John and Sarah will discuss those in advance (if that's possible), Emma will keep the receipts and John and Sarah will reimburse promptly.

At the beginning of the pregnancy, John reviews the budget monthly to see how things are tracking. As he starts to get a feel for what the actual expenses are, John, Sarah and Emma discuss those and make adjustments as they need. John keeps a spreadsheet in a shared document drive, which everyone can access at all times. They catch up every 6 weeks or so to ensure that everyone is on the same page about the budget and actual expenses. This regular communication ensures that everyone is on the same page financially and helps build trust and understanding among all parties involved.

By leveraging John's financial expertise, maintaining clear boundaries and fostering open communication, John, Sarah and Emma successfully navigate the financial aspects of their surrogacy arrangement. They strike a balance between effective budget management and respecting Emma's autonomy, ensuring a supportive and financially secure journey towards welcoming their child into the world.

By proactively addressing financial considerations and implementing effective budgeting strategies, you can navigate the surrogacy journey while limiting the stress and awkwardness that can come from talking about money. Clear communication, careful planning and mutual respect are key pillars in managing surrogacy costs responsibly and ensuring everyone is on the same page.

BUDGETING FOR YOUR SURROGACY

Taking the time to plan and work through expenses allows you to remove some of the stress and anxiety involved in the process. Remember that the more information you have, the more confident you will be able to move through the process. Below is a budget checklist to work through as a guide to ensuring that you have considered all relevant expenses.

Pre-Conception Phase

Medical Expenses	
Fertility treatments (e.g., IVF procedures)	$
Medications related to fertility treatments	$
Medical consultations with fertility specialists	$
Legal Expenses	
Legal advice and consultation fees for both intended parents and birth parents	$
Drafting and reviewing surrogacy agreement	$

Preparation of legal documents required by the court	$
Counselling	
Counselling sessions for intended parents and birth parents as required by Queensland law	$
Counselling to prepare for emotional and psychological aspects of surrogacy	$

Pregnancy Phase

Medical Expenses	
Antenatal care and obstetrician fees	$
Pregnancy-related medical tests and screenings	$
Ultrasound scans and other medical imaging	$
Living Expenses	
Reimbursement for reasonable living expenses incurred by the surrogate during pregnancy (e.g., maternity clothing, travel to medical appointments)	$
Insurance	
Health insurance coverage for the surrogate, if applicable	$

Birth Phase

Delivery Expenses	
Hospital or birthing centre fees	$
Obstetrician or midwife fees for delivery	$
Postnatal Care	
Postnatal medical care for the surrogate	$
Postnatal care for the child, if applicable	$

Legal and Administrative Costs

Parentage Order Application	
Legal fees for applying for a parentage order	$
Court filing fees and other legal administrative costs	$
Birth Registration	
Fees associated with registering the birth of the child with Births, Deaths and Marriages Queensland	$
Updating legal documents such as birth certificates after the parentage order is granted	$

Contingency Fund

Unexpected Expenses	
Emergency medical expenses for birth mother or child	$
Unforeseen legal or counselling expenses	$

Tips for Managing the Surrogacy Budget

1. Create a timeline and budget spreadsheet to track expenses throughout the process.
2. Maintain open communication with the surrogate and any professionals involved to anticipate costs and plan accordingly.
3. Consider setting up a separate bank account or fund specifically for surrogacy-related expenses to manage finances efficiently.
4. Ensure all expenses reimbursed to the surrogate comply with Queensland laws and regulations regarding surrogacy.

"Begin as you mean to go on" is apt when setting yourself up for a successful surrogacy. Have a plan, think carefully through the costs, be realistic and think about your worst-case scenario and just how expensive the process may become. When you have these things in your mind, you will be better able to adapt to whatever happens on your surrogacy journey.

CONCLUDING THOUGHTS

As you embark on your path to surrogacy, it's crucial to recognise the various financial considerations and plan accordingly. By understanding the costs involved, budgeting effectively and exploring financial support options, you can approach your surrogacy process with greater confidence.

My key takeaways are these:

1. Surrogacy involves a range of financial expenses, including medical fees, legal costs and other reimbursements for the birth mother. Create a budget and share it with the birth mother and her spouse. By knowing all potential expenses and being open about them, you can plan effectively and avoid unexpected financial burdens along the way.
2. When creating your budget, be realistic. Consider your worst-case scenario so that when unexpected expenses arise, you can roll with it and focus on the big picture.
3. Clear and honest communication between all parties is essential for managing costs effectively. You can avoid misunderstandings by discussing expectations around costs, how those expenses will be reimbursed and managing the day-to-day.

What are your key takeaways? Pull out your highlighter and sticky tabs, or make some notes below.

Chapter 6:

Looking After Yourself

The surrogacy process comes with its share of emotional challenges and stressors for both intended parents and birth parents. Recognising the importance of emotional well-being, this chapter explores the various avenues through which you can find support, guidance and ultimately look after yourself as you navigate the complexities of surrogacy.

Attending counselling is a compulsory part of the surrogacy journey, with the need for pre-surrogacy counselling and then the preparation of a surrogacy guidance report. The emotional complexities of the surrogacy process, however, often require additional support from mental health professionals. Therapy can play a pivotal role in helping intended parents and birth parents navigate the emotional challenges, uncertainties and joys associated with surrogacy.

Looking after yourself extends to self-care, self-compassion and setting boundaries. The surrogacy process can become all-consuming if you allow it to be. In this chapter, we work through the benefits of taking time out for yourself and giving yourself a break in order to not just survive but thrive in this process.

Building on the themes of resilience, empathy and connection, this chapter emphasises the significance of creating a robust support network of friends, family, professionals and like-minded individuals who can offer unwavering support and compassion. From providing practical assistance to lending a listening ear, these networks play a crucial role in providing comfort and encouragement during both the highs and lows of the surrogacy journey.

By tapping into all of these resources, you can access support services, specialised guidance and connections to foster resilience, empowerment and ultimately look after yourself during your surrogacy journey.

THE ROLE OF THERAPY BEYOND THE LEGAL REQUIREMENTS FOR REPORTS

Beyond the legal requirements, therapy provides an opportunity for intended parents and birth parents to foster a deeper understanding of each other's perspectives, build trust and rapport and strengthen their relationship throughout the surrogacy process. By engaging in therapy, you can develop coping strategies, enhance communication skills and cultivate resilience to navigate the emotional ups and downs of surrogacy.

Therapy offers a number of benefits for all parties involved in the surrogacy arrangement to express their feelings, address concerns and explore their emotions openly. Intended parents may experience a range of emotions, including anxiety, excitement and apprehension, as they embark on the journey to parenthood through surrogacy. Similarly, birth parents may grapple with their own set of emotions, from altruistic motivations to feelings of attachment and fulfilment.

Therapy provides a **supportive and confidential space** for you to navigate complex emotions and challenges associated with surrogacy. For intended parents, this may include addressing feelings of anxiety, guilt, or uncertainty about the surrogacy process. You can explore your expectations, fears and hopes related to becoming parents through surrogacy, which can be especially valuable if you have faced infertility or pregnancy loss in the past. Therapy helps you gain clarity, build resilience and develop coping strategies to manage stress effectively throughout the journey.

Birth parents benefit from therapy by addressing their unique emotional and psychological needs. Pregnancy, whether it's one's own or as a surrogate, can evoke a range of emotions, from joy and fulfilment to anxiety and physical discomfort. Therapy provides birth parents with **a space to process these emotions openly and without judgment**. It helps you navigate the complexities of carrying a child for someone else, including feelings of attachment, identity and the impact on your own family dynamics.

Therapy **enhances communication and fosters healthier relationships** between all parties. It encourages open dialogue, empathy and understanding, which are crucial for maintaining trust and mutual respect throughout the process. Therapy sessions often involve exploring boundaries, expectations and roles, ensuring that everyone's needs and concerns are acknowledged and addressed proactively.

Therapy can also equip you with **practical tools and strategies to cope with challenges** that may arise during the surrogacy journey. This could include managing conflicts, making informed decisions and adjusting to unexpected outcomes or changes in plans. Therapists specialising in surrogacy understand the unique dynamics involved and can offer tailored guidance and support based on your individual circumstances and needs.

Case Study: Tabitha, Stewart and Cathy

Meet Tabitha and Stewart, who have been struggling with infertility for several years due to medical complications. After exhausting various fertility treatments without success, they decided to pursue surrogacy. They connected with a surrogate, Cathy, who graciously offered to carry a child for them.

During the pregnancy phase, Tabitha and Stewart found themselves experiencing a range of emotions. While they were thrilled about the prospect of becoming parents, they also grappled with anxiety and uncertainty. Tabitha often felt guilty about not being able to carry the baby herself and worried about Cathy's well-being during the pregnancy. Stewart, on the other hand, struggled with feelings of helplessness and fear of the unknown.

Recognising the emotional toll of the surrogacy journey, Tabitha and Stewart decided to seek counselling. They attended sessions together to address their concerns, manage stress and strengthen their communication skills. The counsellor provided them with a safe space to express their feelings and validated their experiences. Through therapy, Tabitha and Stewart learned coping strategies to navigate the ups and downs of the pregnancy phase. They also developed a deeper understanding of the importance of self-care and supporting Cathy throughout her pregnancy.

Counselling helped Tabitha and Stewart cultivate a positive mindset and fostered a strong bond with Cathy. They gained reassurance that their feelings were valid and normal for intended parents in surrogacy arrangements. By proactively addressing their emotional needs, Tabitha and Stewart were better equipped to support each other and Cathy during the pregnancy phase.

Case Study: Alex and Jamie, Frankie and Mark

Meet Alex and Jamie, who decided to become birth parents for their close friends, Frankie and Mark. Jamie, who is carrying the child for Frankie and Mark, underwent the embryo transfer successfully and is now in the early stages of pregnancy.

Throughout this early stage, Jamie's spouse, Alex, experienced a mix of emotions. While he was supportive of Jamie's decision to carry the baby for their friends, he also faced his own set of challenges. Alex often grappled with feelings of being left out of the physical experience of pregnancy and very much "along for the ride" and struggled to adjust to the changes in their relationship dynamics.

Despite Alex's unwavering support for Jamie and their friends, he found it helpful to seek someone to talk to during this time. Alex reached out to a counsellor specialising in surrogacy and reproductive issues. In counselling sessions, Alex expressed his concerns about navigating his role as the spouse of a surrogate, managing his emotions and maintaining a healthy relationship with Jamie.

The counsellor provided Alex with a safe and confidential space to discuss his feelings and fears without judgment. In counselling sessions, they explored coping strategies to address feelings of isolation and uncertainty and techniques to strengthen his bond with Jamie throughout the pregnancy. The counsellor also emphasised the importance of self-care for Alex and encouraged open communication with Jamie about his emotions and needs.

Alex gained perspective and reassurance that his feelings were valid and common among spouses of surrogates. He learned practical ways to support Jamie effectively while also taking care of his own emotional well-being. Ultimately, counselling helped Alex navigate the complexities of the pregnancy stage, fostering a deeper connection with Jamie and strengthening their partnership in supporting their friends' surrogacy journey.

SELF-CARE, SELF-COMPASSION AND THE IMPORTANCE OF BOUNDARIES

Self-care is essential for all parties involved in a surrogacy arrangement, as the journey can be emotionally and physically demanding. For intended parents, navigating the complexities of surrogacy – from legal and financial obligations to the emotional highs and lows – can be overwhelming.

Self-care practices provide a crucial foundation for maintaining resilience and well-being throughout this process. It allows you to manage stress, stay emotionally grounded and nurture your mental health, ensuring you can effectively support your surrogate and yourself.

Similarly, birth parents also face unique challenges. The birth mother undergoes physical changes and emotional transitions during pregnancy, coupled with the responsibility of carrying a child for someone else. Self-care activities become essential for managing physical health, addressing emotional needs and maintaining a positive mindset. By prioritising self-care, surrogates can sustain their energy levels, manage any discomfort associated with pregnancy and cultivate a supportive environment for themselves and their families.

In the following section, we will explore practical examples of self-care activities for both intended parents and birth parents. These activities promote overall well-being, reduce stress and foster a supportive environment conducive to a successful surrogacy journey. Whether through relaxation techniques, physical exercise, or emotional outlets, integrating self-care practices into daily life ensures that all parties can navigate the surrogacy process with resilience and compassion.

Intended Parents

Maintain **open and honest communication** with your partner and the birth parents throughout the process. Discuss your feelings, concerns and hopes and seek emotional support from each other and trusted friends or family members.

Stay informed about the surrogacy journey by reading reputable sources, attending support groups or workshops and connecting with other intended parents who have gone through similar experiences.

Prioritise your **physical health** by engaging in regular exercise, eating nutritious meals and getting enough rest. Physical activity can help manage stress and improve overall well-being during this challenging time.

Practice **mindfulness techniques** such as meditation, deep breathing exercises, or yoga to reduce stress levels and promote relaxation. Carving out time for these practices can provide a sense of calm amidst the complexities of the surrogacy process.

Dedicate time to **activities that bring you joy and fulfilment** outside of the surrogacy journey. Whether it's a hobby, creative outlet, or recreational activity, engaging in something you love can help maintain a balanced perspective.

Birth Parents

Focus on maintaining **good physical health** by attending regular prenatal appointments, following medical advice and adhering to a nutritious diet. Ensure you are getting enough rest and prioritise self-care activities that support your well-being.

Seek emotional support from your support network, including family, friends, or a counsellor if needed. Acknowledge your feelings throughout the process and allow yourself space to process emotions related to pregnancy and surrogacy.

Establish **clear boundaries** with the intended parents and healthcare providers to ensure your needs and preferences are respected throughout the pregnancy. Communicate openly about your expectations and concerns.

Practice **relaxation techniques** such as gentle exercise, prenatal yoga, or mindfulness to alleviate stress and promote relaxation during pregnancy.

Take time to **celebrate milestones in the pregnancy journey**, such as feeling the baby's first movements or reaching significant prenatal appointments. Reflect on the positive impact you are making in helping another family achieve their dream of parenthood.

Taking care of yourself ensures that each party can contribute positively to the experience, fostering a supportive and nurturing environment for all involved.

Self-compassion and setting boundaries are fundamental to successfully navigating a surrogacy arrangement. They are crucial for both intended parents and birth parents. Surrogacy involves complex emotional, physical and legal dynamics that can challenge personal well-being and relationships. For intended parents, self-compassion means acknowledging the difficulties and uncertainties inherent in the process without self-judgment. It allows you to manage expectations, cope with setbacks and maintain a positive outlook throughout the journey. Setting boundaries ensures you protect their emotional energy and maintain healthy relationships with your surrogate, partners and support network.

Similarly, for birth parents, self-compassion involves recognising and honouring their own needs amidst the physical demands of pregnancy and the emotional journey of carrying a child for someone else. Setting boundaries is equally vital, helping you to manage expectations, communicate your needs clearly and navigate the unique challenges of being a surrogate. It empowers the birth mother to prioritise her well-being and advocate for her physical and emotional health throughout the process.

Self-compassion and setting boundaries are crucial for both intended parents and birth parents in a surrogacy arrangement. By understanding these principles and applying them in practical ways, all parties involved can foster healthier relationships, navigate challenges effectively and ensure the well-being of everyone throughout the surrogacy journey.

Intended Parents

Embarking on the surrogacy journey can bring a rollercoaster of emotions, from hope and anticipation to anxiety and uncertainty.

Self-compassion allows intended parents to **acknowledge and validate their feelings without judgment**. It helps them cope with disappointments or setbacks along the way, fostering resilience and perseverance.

Setting boundaries is vital for **maintaining emotional stability and well-being** throughout the surrogacy process. It involves clearly defining expectations, roles and responsibilities with the surrogate and other parties involved. Establishing healthy boundaries ensures that intended parents can prioritise their own needs, communicate effectively and navigate potential challenges with clarity and respect.

Practicing self-compassion **enables intended parents to empathise with the surrogate's experience and challenges**. It encourages a compassionate approach to communication and decision-making, fostering a supportive relationship based on mutual respect and understanding. By setting boundaries, intended parents can uphold the surrogate's autonomy and ensure her physical and emotional well-being are prioritised throughout the pregnancy journey.

Surrogacy involves waiting periods and uncertainties, such as the success of medical procedures or legal processes. Self-compassion helps intended parents **navigate these waiting periods with patience and self-care**. It encourages them to practice mindfulness and resilience, managing stress and anxiety effectively while maintaining a positive outlook.

Birth Parents

Self-compassion allows birth parents to **honour their emotional well-being throughout the pregnancy journey**. It involves acknowledging their feelings, fears and joys without self-criticism. By practicing self-compassion, surrogates can navigate the physical and emotional challenges of pregnancy with greater resilience and acceptance.

Establishing boundaries is crucial for the birth mother to protect her physical health and autonomy during pregnancy. It involves **clearly communicating her needs, preferences and limitations** to the intended parents and healthcare providers. Setting boundaries ensures that surrogates feel respected, supported and empowered throughout the surrogacy process.

Surrogacy requires birth parents to **balance their own well-being with the needs and expectations of the intended parents**. Self-compassion enables the birth mother in particular to prioritise self-care, rest and relaxation, which are essential for a healthy pregnancy. By setting boundaries, birth parents can manage their time, energy and emotional resources effectively, ensuring a positive and fulfilling surrogacy experience.

Self-compassion and setting boundaries are integral to the surrogacy journey for all parties. These practices promote emotional resilience, support healthy relationships and ensure that the needs and well-being of all involved are respected and prioritised throughout the process.

FINDING BALANCE AND MAINTAINING YOUR SANITY

The journey of surrogacy is inherently emotional, both for intended parents and surrogates, as they navigate through a complex process towards a shared goal of bringing a child into the world. While the focus is understandably on the practical aspects – legalities, medical procedures and logistical arrangements – it's equally important to recognise and manage the emotional implications that can arise along the way. One crucial aspect of this journey is **finding a balance that allows you to remain grounded and emotionally resilient without letting the surrogacy process consume your life**.

For intended parents, the emotional rollercoaster begins long before the embryo transfer. Many have endured years of infertility struggles or medical challenges that led them to pursue surrogacy. The anticipation, hope and anxiety that accompany each stage – from selecting a surrogate to waiting for conception and navigating the pregnancy – are intense. These emotions can fluctuate, often influenced by external factors such as the birth mother's health, medical updates and legal procedures. Intended parents may experience a range of feelings, including joy, fear, guilt and even occasional doubts about the outcome.

Birth parents, on the other hand, embark on a journey that requires immense generosity and selflessness. They may have their own emotional challenges, balancing their commitment to help others achieve parenthood with their own family dynamics and personal lives. The pregnancy itself can bring forth a mix of emotions, from pride in their role as a surrogate to concerns about the physical toll and potential emotional attachment to the baby they are carrying. Birth mothers often navigate a delicate balance between maintaining their own health and well-being while supporting the intended parents through this transformative experience.

Finding equilibrium in the surrogacy process involves several key strategies. Firstly, **open and honest communication** between intended parents and the surrogate is paramount. Clear expectations, regular updates and mutual respect foster trust and understanding, mitigating potential misunderstandings or emotional strain. Establishing boundaries – both physical and emotional – helps all parties maintain a healthy perspective and prevent burnout or emotional exhaustion.

Additionally, **self-care practices** are essential for both intended parents and surrogates. This includes prioritising activities that promote relaxation, mindfulness and emotional resilience. Engaging in hobbies, spending quality time with loved ones and seeking professional support through therapy or counselling can provide valuable outlets for processing emotions and gaining perspective.

Furthermore, **acknowledging and validating emotions as they arise is crucial**. Intended parents should feel empowered to express their feelings openly, whether it's excitement, anxiety, or frustration. Birth parents benefit from understanding that their emotional journey is valued and supported, allowing them to navigate the surrogacy process with greater confidence and peace of mind.

Ultimately, **maintaining a balanced approach to surrogacy involves recognising the inherent emotional complexities while actively nurturing mental and emotional well-being**. By prioritising communication, setting boundaries, practising self-care and acknowledging emotions, you can navigate this transformative journey with resilience, empathy and mutual support. This approach not only enhances the surrogacy experience but also fosters lasting bonds and positive outcomes for all involved.

ADDRESSING EMOTIONAL CHALLENGES AND STRESSORS THROUGHOUT THE SURROGACY PROCESS

It is imperative to address the emotional challenges and stressors that may arise throughout the surrogacy process. While surrogacy is a rewarding journey, it can also be emotionally taxing for all parties involved. Intended parents and surrogates may encounter various stressors and emotional hurdles along the way, from the initial stages of planning and preparation to the birth of the child and beyond.

One of the primary emotional challenges in surrogacy is the **uncertainty and anticipation** that comes with the process. Intended parents may experience heightened levels of anxiety and apprehension as they navigate the complexities of surrogacy, including the selection of a surrogate, medical procedures and legal requirements. Similarly, birth mother may grapple with feelings of pressure, responsibility and emotional attachment as she carries the pregnancy for another individual or couple.

The surrogacy journey may also evoke a **range of emotions, including joy, excitement, sadness and fear**. Intended parents may experience moments of joy and gratitude as they anticipate the arrival of their child. At the same time, birth parents may undergo a rollercoaster of emotions as they navigate the physical and emotional aspects of pregnancy and childbirth. Additionally, unexpected challenges, such as medical complications or legal issues, can exacerbate stress and emotional strain for all parties involved.

It's essential for intended parents and surrogates to recognise and address these emotional challenges proactively. Open communication, empathy and mutual support are key in navigating the ups and downs of the surrogacy journey. Seeking guidance from mental health professionals, engaging in therapy sessions and participating in support groups can provide valuable emotional support and coping strategies to manage stress, enhance resilience and foster positive outcomes for everyone involved in the surrogacy process.

CREATE A SUPPORTIVE NETWORK OF FRIENDS, FAMILIES AND PROFESSIONALS.

Building a support system of friends, family and professionals can provide invaluable emotional guidance, reassurance and understanding for both intended parents and surrogates as they navigate the complexities of the surrogacy process.

First and foremost, you should **lean on your immediate support**

networks, including family members, close friends and loved ones. This inner circle offers unconditional love, encouragement and practical assistance during challenging times, serving as pillars of strength and sources of comfort throughout the surrogacy journey. Whether it's lending a listening ear, helping with household tasks, or providing emotional support, a supportive network can make a significant difference in alleviating stress and fostering a sense of connection and belonging.

Additionally, **seeking guidance and support from experienced professionals**, such as fertility clinics and mental health professionals, can be instrumental in navigating the emotional complexities of surrogacy. There are comprehensive support services available from services who provide dedicated surrogacy advice to assist at every step of the process. Surrogacy counselling services can provide you with specific guidance or a referral to specialised assistance. Your lawyer will likely have connections to point you in the right direction. Fertility clinics offer specialised medical expertise and emotional support to help individuals and couples achieve their family-building goals through surrogacy.

Joining surrogacy **support groups and online communities** can also offer a sense of camaraderie and solidarity for individuals and couples embarking on the surrogacy journey. These forums provide a safe space for sharing experiences, seeking advice and connecting with others who understand the unique challenges and triumphs of surrogacy. By engaging with peers who have walked a similar path, you can find solace, encouragement and validation, fostering a sense of empowerment and resilience as you navigate the emotional ups and downs of surrogacy.

CONCLUDING THOUGHTS

This process will be filled with ups and downs and significant stress and anxiety as you manage all of the medical, legal and financial competing priorities. Seeking support is essential. Get counselling, talk to friends and family and join support groups. Ensure that you have the support you need to navigate the complexities of surrogacy with resilience, empathy and confidence.

Here are my three key takeaways:

1. Surround yourself with a diverse network of friends, family and professionals. Online communities provide a vital source of comfort, guidance and understanding. Cultivate connections so you can lean on others for emotional support during the good times and the bad.
2. A wealth of resources exists to support individuals on their surrogacy journey, whether through counselling services or your fertility clinic. Explore these resources and you will find the tools and assistance to navigate emotional challenges effectively.
3. It's essential for you to prioritise self-care and emotional well-being. Go for a walk or exercise, but more importantly, be kind to yourself, set boundaries and engage in activities that bring joy and relaxation.

What are your key takeaways? Pull out your highlighter and sticky tabs, or make some notes below.

Chapter 7:

Practical Considerations for the Surrogacy Journey and Beyond

Practicality and foresight play pivotal roles in ensuring a smooth and successful process. Being mindful of the practical aspects and considerations, from honouring the birth mother to managing the various tasks and challenges that arise, will help you navigate the path ahead.

Open communication, remaining positive and asking for help are essential. Throughout this chapter, we emphasise the importance of maintaining open communication, fostering positive relationships and seeking support from both professionals and loved ones. Whether it's establishing a respectful and supportive relationship with the surrogate, navigating the surrogacy journey with practical tips, or considering post-surrogacy considerations, we aim to equip intended parents with the knowledge and tools they need to navigate this transformative experience with confidence and grace.

By embracing practicality, compassion and resilience, intended parents can approach the surrogacy journey with a sense of preparedness and empowerment. As we delve into the practical tips and considerations outlined in this chapter, we invite readers to embark on this journey with an open heart and a readiness to embrace the challenges and joys that lie ahead.

NAVIGATING THE SURROGACY JOURNEY

Navigating the surrogacy journey requires careful planning, organisation and preparation. Here are some practical tips and considerations to help intended parents manage the various aspects of the process.

With multiple medical appointments, legal requirements and administrative tasks involved in the surrogacy process, it's essential to **stay organised and proactive**. You should communicate clearly with your fertility clinic, legal advisors and surrogacy agency (if applicable) to ensure all necessary appointments and tasks are scheduled and completed on time. Keeping detailed records of medical records, legal documents and correspondence can help streamline the process and prevent oversights or delays.

Developing a **comprehensive timeline and checklist** can help you stay on track and ensure no important steps are overlooked. Begin by outlining key milestones and deadlines, such as medical screenings, legal consultations, surrogate matching, embryo transfer and birth registration. Break down each milestone into actionable steps and set realistic timelines for completion. Regularly review and update the timeline and checklist as the surrogacy journey progresses, adjusting as needed to accommodate any changes or developments.

While the surrogacy journey can be incredibly rewarding, it may also present various challenges or obstacles along the way. You should approach the process with flexibility, resilience and a proactive mindset, anticipating potential issues and planning accordingly. This may involve **researching potential legal hurdles, understanding the emotional complexities of the journey and seeking support from experienced professionals or support networks**. By being prepared to address challenges as they arise, intended parents can navigate the surrogacy journey with confidence and clarity.

Case Study: Samantha, Jason and Elise

Samantha and Jason, an intended parent couple, had carefully planned their surrogacy journey with their surrogate, Elise. They had completed all legal requirements, undergone counselling and were eagerly making their way through the pregnancy phase after successful embryo transfer. However, during a routine prenatal check-up at the 20-week mark, Elise's obstetrician discovered a previously undetected medical condition that could potentially complicate the remainder of the pregnancy.

The unexpected complication raised concerns for Samantha, Jason and Elise about the health and well-being of both Elise and the baby. Samantha and Jason found themselves grappling with feelings of anxiety and uncertainty, as their initial excitement turned into worry about the potential risks and outcomes of the pregnancy.

Elise, on the other hand, faced emotional challenges related to her role as a surrogate. She felt torn between her commitment to help Samantha and Jason become parents and her own health concerns. The unexpected medical complication added an additional layer of stress, as she navigated her own fears while also wanting to provide reassurance and support to the intended parents.

In response to this unforeseen challenge, all parties involved – Samantha, Jason, Elise and the medical team – came together to discuss the next steps. They sought guidance from counsellors and medical professionals to better understand the implications of the medical condition and explore options to ensure the best possible outcome for both Elise and the baby.

Therapy sessions became crucial during this period, helping Samantha and Jason express their concerns openly and receive emotional support. They discussed their fears of potential complications and the impact on their dream of becoming parents. Elise utilised therapy to process her own emotions, including feelings of guilt and worry about the surrogate pregnancy.

Through therapy and open communication facilitated by their counsellors, Samantha, Jason and Elise were able to navigate this unexpected medical complication. They adjusted their expectations and plans accordingly, focusing on supporting Elise's health while maintaining their shared goal of a healthy pregnancy and birth. They agreed to a plan that prioritised Elise's health in the event their were any complications as the pregnancy continued.

Despite careful planning, unexpected challenges can arise, requiring all parties to communicate effectively, seek professional guidance and prioritise the well-being of everyone involved in the surrogacy journey.

While planning is essential for ensuring all parties involved are prepared and informed, it's equally important to recognise that life can present unexpected challenges that may require flexibility and adaptation.

Despite the best land and thorough planning, life often unfolds in unforeseen ways. Personal or family emergencies, health issues, or other unexpected events can arise that impact the surrogacy journey. For intended parents, these challenges may affect their ability to participate fully or require adjustments to their roles and responsibilities. For birth parents, unexpected health concerns or personal circumstances may temporarily delay the process or necessitate additional support.

Understanding the need to roll with life's challenges involves maintaining flexibility and adaptability throughout the surrogacy journey. This mindset acknowledges that despite careful planning, circumstances can change and adjustments may be necessary. It encourages open communication and collaboration between all parties to navigate unexpected situations effectively.

Embracing flexibility in surrogacy enhances resilience and strengthens relationships between intended parents and surrogates. It fosters a supportive environment where challenges are addressed constructively and solutions are sought collaboratively. It also reinforces the understanding that surrogacy is a shared journey requiring empathy, understanding and mutual respect.

While planning is essential, recognising the inevitability of life's uncertainties is equally crucial. Intended parents and surrogates should approach this journey with the understand that unforeseen challenges may arise.

POST-SURROGACY CONSIDERATIONS

Post-surrogacy considerations are crucial for intended parents as they transition into parenthood and navigate the complexities of their new family dynamic. Here are some essential factors to consider.

Welcoming a child into the family through surrogacy is a joyous and life-changing experience, but it can also be overwhelming. Intended parents may need time to adjust to their new roles and responsibilities as parents and bond with their child. **Taking things one day at a time**, seeking support from loved ones and being patient with oneself are essential during this period of adjustment.

Even after the child's birth, the relationship between the intended parents and the birth parents remains important. **Continuing to offer the surrogate emotional support, gratitude and appreciation** can help maintain a positive relationship and ensure ongoing communication and connection. Intended parents should also be mindful of the surrogate's emotional needs and well-being, offering support as needed during her postpartum recovery.

The surrogacy journey doesn't end with the birth of the child; rather, it evolves into a new chapter of parenthood and family life. **Seeking ongoing therapy, assistance and advice can be beneficial for both the intended parents and the birth parents** as they navigate the joys and challenges of post-surrogacy life. Whether addressing any lingering emotional concerns, seeking guidance on parenting issues, or simply having someone to talk to, professional support can help ensure a smoother transition and a healthier family unit.

Fostering openness and honesty about the child's birth parentage is paramount for the child's well-being and best interests in the post-surrogacy journey. This ongoing process involves intentional conversations and efforts from both intended parents and birth parents to nurture bonds and relationships that honour the child's unique family dynamics.

Communication forms the foundation of promoting openness and honesty in surrogacy arrangements. Intended parents and birth parents should initiate **age-appropriate conversations with the child about their surrogacy journey from an early age**. This can begin with simple explanations tailored to the child's developmental stage, gradually evolving into more detailed discussions as they grow older.

For example, using storybooks or visual aids that depict different family structures can help normalise the concept of surrogacy for young children. Creating a photobook of the surrogacy journey is a way that parties can capture and honour the process and the part each person played. These tools can facilitate discussions about how the child was born and the roles of the birth mother and intended parents in their life.

Transparency about the surrogacy arrangement should be maintained throughout the child's life. Both sets of parents can regularly share updates and milestones with each other, ensuring that the child grows up with a clear understanding of their biological origins and the loving intentions behind their conception and birth.

This might include annual meetings, video calls, or written updates exchanged between intended parents and birth parents. You can arrange inclusive family celebrations, where both sets of parents are acknowledged and included in important events such as birthdays, holidays and milestones in the child's life.

For example, organising joint family gatherings or special outings that involve both sets of parents can reinforce the child's sense of belonging and connection to their extended family. These shared experiences create lasting memories and reinforce the positive impact of openness and collaboration in surrogacy arrangements.

Navigating the complexities of post-surrogacy relationships **may require ongoing professional support and guidance**. Intended parents and birth parents can benefit from seeking advice from counsellors or therapists experienced in surrogacy dynamics. These professionals can provide tools for effective communication, assist in managing emotions and offer strategies for maintaining healthy relationships over time.

By considering these post-surrogacy factors and prioritising ongoing support, communication and self-care, intended parents can navigate the transition into parenthood with confidence, compassion and resilience.

CONCLUDING THOUGHTS

In concluding this chapter, it's clear that navigating the surrogacy journey requires a blend of practicality, empathy and resilience. By incorporating these key principles into their approach, intended parents can better navigate the complexities and challenges that accompany the surrogacy process.

My three key takeaways are these:

1. Maintaining open and respectful communication with all parties involved is paramount throughout the surrogacy journey. By honouring the birth mother's contribution, providing support and expressing gratitude, intended parents can foster positive relationships that contribute to a smoother and more fulfilling experience.

2. Managing the surrogacy journey involves a myriad of tasks and responsibilities, from medical appointments to legal obligations. By creating a timeline, checklist and anticipating potential obstacles, intended parents can stay organised and proactive, reducing stress and ensuring that nothing falls through the cracks.
3. The journey doesn't end with the birth of the child. Intended parents must adjust to parenthood, continue supporting the surrogate and seek ongoing therapy and assistance as needed. By recognising the importance of post-surrogacy considerations and maintaining a supportive network, intended parents can navigate this transitional period with grace.

What are your key takeaways? Pull out your highlighter and sticky tabs, or make some notes below.

Conclusion

Thank you for reading our guide on Surrogacy in Queensland. To conclude this book, I want to highlight some key messages to take with you on your own surrogacy journey.

A thorough grasp of the legal framework is fundamental to confidently navigating this journey. Understanding the legal requirement ensures compliance from the outset, setting a solid foundation for the entire process.

Each surrogacy journey is as unique as the individuals involved, necessitating a nuanced approach to eligibility requirements that considers the specific circumstances of each party involved. This personalised assessment ensures that all aspects of the surrogacy arrangement are properly addressed and accounted for.

Chapter 3 of our guide serves as a structured roadmap, guiding you through the ten critical steps to a successful surrogacy journey in Queensland. By systematically addressing each step, from establishing a social or medical need to obtaining a parentage order, this approach equips you with comprehensive insights and practical strategies. This detailed understanding empowers you to make informed decisions at every stage, mitigating uncertainties and fostering confidence.

Communicate well. Clear and open dialogue among all parties involved is essential for fostering trust, resolving potential issues and ensuring alignment of expectations. Miscommunication or lack thereof can lead to misunderstandings or conflicts, underscoring the importance of proactive and transparent communication throughout the journey.

Financial considerations are significant but require a balanced approach. While it's crucial to have a clear understanding of the financial implications associated with surrogacy, including reimbursing expenses and managing a budget, flexibility is also key. All parties should be prepared for unexpected costs or changes in circumstances, allowing for adjustments without compromising the integrity of the surrogacy arrangement.

Self-care is another critical component of navigating the emotional and practical challenges inherent in the surrogacy process. Practising self-compassion, setting boundaries and managing expectations are vital for maintaining emotional well-being and resilience. This self-awareness and proactive approach contribute to a healthier and more positive surrogacy experience for all involved.

While planning is essential for ensuring that all parties involved are prepared and informed, it is equally important to recognise that life can expect unexpected challenges that may require flexibility and the need to adapt.

I set out with the aim of providing you with the knowledge, tools and resources needed to navigate this process successfully. It has always been my philosophy in life and law that the more information you have and the more informed you are about the issue you are navigating, the more empowered you are to make good decisions for your future.

On that note, I wish you all the very best with your surrogacy journey.

Elizabeth

Resources

PRECONCEPTION CHECKLIST FOR SURROGACY

The surrogacy journey can be complex, with medical, emotional and legal matters to manage. It is helpful to have a checklist to ensure all necessary steps and considerations are addressed before pressing ahead. When you plan, you help to avoid risks, communicate well, clarify the expectations of all parties and lay a solid foundation for a successful surrogacy experience for all parties involved.

Here are some key factors you should work through before formalising your conception process.

- [ ] **Medical Assessment**: Undergo comprehensive medical assessments to determine eligibility for surrogacy, including fertility evaluations and health screenings.
- [ ] **Surrogate Selection**: Explore options for finding a suitable surrogate, whether through agencies, personal connections, or online platforms and conduct thorough screenings and interviews.

- [ ] **Counselling**: Attend pre-surrogacy counselling sessions with the surrogate and all intended parents to ensure everyone fully understands the emotional, psychological and legal aspects of the arrangement.
- [ ] **Parental Planning**: Consider and discuss important aspects of parenthood, such as parenting styles, involvement in the child's life and plans for any potential future children.
- [ ] **Communication and Consent**: Maintain open and honest communication with all parties involved, ensuring everyone's consent and understanding of their roles and responsibilities in the surrogacy arrangement.
- [ ] **Financial Planning**: Assess and plan for the financial costs involved in the surrogacy process, including medical expenses, legal fees, counselling fees and any reimbursements for the birth mother.
- [ ] **Emotional Preparedness**: Prepare emotionally for the surrogacy journey, understanding that it may involve challenges, uncertainties and complex emotions for all parties involved.
- [ ] **Medical and Legal Documentation**: Gather all necessary medical records and legal documentation required for the surrogacy process, including medical histories, consent forms and financial agreements.
- [ ] **Surrogacy Agreement**: Work with legal professionals to draft a comprehensive surrogacy agreement outlining all terms and conditions, including rights, responsibilities, compensation and expectations of all parties involved.

- [ ] **Legal Consultation**: Seek legal advice to understand the legal implications, rights and responsibilities associated with surrogacy arrangements in your jurisdiction.
- [ ] **Support System**: Build a strong support network of family, friends and professionals who can provide emotional support and guidance throughout the surrogacy journey.
- [ ] **Continued Education**: Stay informed about surrogacy laws, regulations and best practices and continue to educate yourself on relevant topics throughout the surrogacy process.

PRACTICAL TOOLS FOR THE BIRTH MOTHER

While there are many aspects of the surrogacy journey to manage and the intended parents undergo significant medical intervention, the birth mother plays the pivotal role that goes beyond the physical act of carrying a child. Having practical tools and resources is essential for navigating this intricate journey.

Here are some examples of practical checklists or tools that can assist the birth mother throughout the surrogacy journey:

1. **Medical Appointments Tracker**: A detailed calendar or spreadsheet to keep track of all medical appointments, including prenatal visits, ultrasounds and check-ups with fertility specialists or obstetricians.
2. **Medication Schedule**: A checklist or reminder system to ensure timely administration of medications prescribed during the surrogacy process, such as hormone injections or supplements.
3. **Health Journal**: A journal or log to record personal health observations, including any symptoms, changes in diet or exercise and general well-being throughout the pregnancy.
4. **Surrogacy Agreement Checklist**: A checklist outlining key provisions and milestones in the surrogacy agreement, including legal obligations, financial arrangements and expectations for communication with intended parents.
5. **Financial Tracker**: A budgeting tool to monitor expenses related to the surrogacy journey, such as medical bills, travel costs, maternity clothing and other incidental expenses. This ensures reimbursement for eligible expenses as per the agreement.
6. **Emotional Well-being Planner**: A resource to track emotional well-being and stress levels, with prompts for self-care activities, counselling sessions, or support group meetings

to maintain mental health throughout the process.

7. **Contact Log**: A log to document communication with intended parents, including emails, phone calls and in-person meetings. This helps maintain clear records of discussions and agreements reached during the journey.
8. **Birth Plan Outline**: A template or checklist to outline preferences for labour and delivery, including medical interventions, birth preferences and postpartum considerations. This ensures all parties are informed and aligned regarding the birth experience.
9. **Legal Document Organiser**: A folder or digital repository to store copies of legal documents related to the surrogacy arrangement, including the surrogacy agreement, parental orders, medical consent forms and any legal correspondence.
10. **Post-Birth Care Plan**: A plan outlining post-birth arrangements, such as lactation support (if applicable), recovery plans and ongoing communication with intended parents regarding the baby's care and well-being.

These practical tools and checklists are designed to support the birth mother in being organised and clear in the process while maintaining her peace of mind in managing all of the competing factors.

PRACTICAL TIPS FOR THE BIRTH MOTHER'S SPOUSE

Navigating the surrogacy journey as the spouse of the birth mother can be both rewarding and challenging. While the birth mother may have a more direct physical and emotional connection to the process, your role as her spouse is crucial in providing support, understanding and practical assistance throughout this experience.

This guide aims to equip you with practical tips to actively participate in and enrich the surrogacy journey alongside your spouse.

1. **Educate Yourself**: Take the initiative to learn about the surrogacy process, including legal aspects, medical procedures and emotional considerations. This will help you understand your role and support your spouse better.
2. **Communicate Openly**: Maintain open communication with your spouse throughout the journey. Discuss your feelings, concerns and expectations regularly to ensure you both feel supported and aligned.
3. **Attend Appointments**: Accompany your spouse to medical appointments, counselling sessions and any meetings with the intended parents. Your presence shows solidarity and reinforces your commitment to the journey.
4. **Offer Practical Support**: Take on practical tasks such as arranging transportation to appointments, organising paperwork and managing household responsibilities to alleviate stress from your spouse.
5. **Emotional Support**: Be attentive to your spouse's emotional needs. Listen actively, provide reassurance and offer comfort during moments of uncertainty or anxiety.
6. **Stay Informed**: Stay updated on the progress of the pregnancy and the overall surrogacy journey. Ask questions and seek

clarification from healthcare providers and counsellors to stay informed.

7. **Bond with the Intended Parents**: Build a positive relationship with the intended parents if possible. Attend meetings together, participate in discussions about the baby's future and foster mutual respect and understanding.
8. **Self-Care**: Prioritise your own well-being by practicing self-care techniques such as exercise, hobbies and relaxation activities. Taking care of yourself ensures you have the energy and resilience to support your spouse effectively.
9. **Celebrate Milestones**: Acknowledge and celebrate important milestones during the pregnancy, such as ultrasound appointments, baby showers (if applicable) and other significant events. These moments strengthen your connection to the journey.
10. **Prepare for Parenthood**: Use this time to prepare for parenthood emotionally and practically. While it is the intended parents who will ultimately be the child's parents, having an understanding about parenting values and goals will assist in maintain a positive relationship with the intended parents beyond the birth of the child.

By actively engaging in these practical tips, the birth mother's spouse can play an integral role in the surrogacy journey, fostering a supportive environment for their spouse and contributing positively to the experience of bringing a child into the world for the intended parents.

PRACTICAL TIPS FOR THE INTENDED PARENTS

Embarking on the journey of surrogacy as intended parents is a transformative experience. It's a path filled with hope, challenges and, ultimately, the promise of growing your family in a unique and meaningful way. Practical guidance can be invaluable to navigate this journey successfully. Here, we explore 10 essential tips tailored to support you through every step of the surrogacy process.

1. **Understanding the Process:** Educating yourselves about the intricacies of surrogacy is crucial. From legal requirements to medical procedures, having a comprehensive understanding will empower you to make informed decisions.
2. **Selecting the Right Surrogate:** It is key to choose a surrogate who shares your values and expectations. Consider factors such as medical history, personality compatibility and communication style when making this important decision.
3. **Building a Strong Relationship:** It is fundamental to have a trusting and open relationship with the birth mother. Clear and respectful communication from the outset lays the foundation for a supportive partnership throughout the journey.
4. **Active Participation:** Engage actively in the surrogacy process by attending medical appointments, legal consultations and counselling sessions. Your presence demonstrates commitment and fosters a collaborative approach.
5. **Creating a Support System:** Surround yourselves with a network of supportive individuals who understand and respect your surrogacy journey. Seek guidance from professionals, friends and family members who can offer emotional support and practical advice.
6. **Financial Planning:** Prepare financially by understanding the

costs associated with surrogacy. Budget for medical expenses, legal fees and any compensation or reimbursement for the surrogate's expenses per legal guidelines.

7. **Emotional Preparedness:** Prepare yourselves emotionally for the highs and lows of the surrogacy journey. Anticipate challenges and lean on your support network for guidance and encouragement throughout.
8. **Respecting Boundaries:** Respect the boundaries set by your surrogate regarding her privacy, medical decisions and involvement in the pregnancy. Clear communication and mutual respect are essential for a positive relationship.
9. **Parental Preparation:** While your surrogate carries the pregnancy, take proactive steps to prepare for parenthood. Attend parenting classes, create a nursery and discuss parenting philosophies to ensure readiness for the baby's arrival.
10. **Celebrating Milestones:** Celebrate important milestones such as ultrasounds, baby showers and the birth of your child with the birth mother. Express gratitude for her invaluable role in helping you achieve your dream of expanding your family.

These practical tips are designed to support you in navigating the complexities of surrogacy with clarity, compassion and resilience. By embracing these guidelines, you can approach the surrogacy journey with confidence, knowing you are equipped to build a strong and positive relationship with the birth mother while preparing for the joy of parenthood ahead.

PARENTAGE APPLICATION CHECKLIST FOR SURROGACY

This checklist is an essential tool designed to guide intended parents through the final stages of the surrogacy journey in Queensland. This checklist ensures that all necessary documents and requirements are meticulously prepared and organised before submitting the application for a parentage order. By following this checklist, you can confidently navigate the legal process and ensure you have complied with the requirements of the Surrogacy Act. This planning will assist in a smooth transition to legal parenthood.

- [ ] **Child's Birth Certificate:** Obtain a certified copy of the child's birth certificate from the relevant authorities.
- [ ] **Surrogacy Arrangement:** Provide a copy of the surrogacy arrangement document outlining the terms and conditions agreed upon by all parties involved.
- [ ] **Affidavit of Applicant(s) (Section 26):** Prepare and swear an affidavit under Section 26 of the Surrogacy Act detailing the applicant's personal circumstances and reasons for seeking a parentage order.
- [ ] **Affidavit of Birth Mother (Section 27):** Obtain an affidavit sworn by the birth mother outlining her understanding and consent to the surrogacy arrangement.
- [ ] **Affidavit of Birth Mother's Spouse (if applicable) (Section 28):** If the birth mother has a spouse, ensure they provide an affidavit affirming their awareness and agreement to the surrogacy arrangement.

- [ ] **Affidavit of Another Birth Parent (if applicable) (Section 29):** If there is another birth parent involved, secure their affidavit confirming their understanding and consent to the surrogacy arrangement.
- [ ] **Affidavit of Legal Advice (Section 30):** Obtain an affidavit from the legal advisor(s) who provided legal counsel to the birth mother, her spouse (if any) and the applicant(s) before the surrogacy arrangement was finalised.
- [ ] **Affidavit of Pre-Surrogacy Counselling (Section 31):** Obtain an affidavit from the qualified counsellors who conducted pre-surrogacy counselling sessions for the birth mother, her spouse (if any) and the applicant(s).
- [ ] **Affidavit Verifying Surrogacy Guidance Report (Section 32):** Obtain an affidavit from the counsellors who prepared the surrogacy guidance report, verifying its contents and authenticity.
- [ ] **Affidavit of Medical Practitioner for Eligible Woman (if applicable):** If any of the applicants are women, secure an affidavit from a qualified medical practitioner verifying the applicant's eligibility as a woman under the Surrogacy Act.

Ensure all documents are complete, accurate and properly sworn before submitting them to the court for the parentage application process.

About the Author

Elizabeth Fairon is a Legal Practice Director at **Life Law Solutions**, with offices in Brisbane, the Sunshine Coast and Hervey Bay. Elizabeth's passion lies with helping families resolve their legal issues, from the creation of families through surrogacy arrangements, assisting families through separation or divorce or resolving disputes within families arising out of the death of a loved one.

Elizabeth is the author of three guides in family law:

- *Trust Yourself*: How empowered decision making will help you resolve your family law matter
- *Love Law*: What to know before you say 'I do'
- *Divorce by Design*: Empowering yourself through conscious choices.

Elizabeth is also the author of *Thrive: A guide for new lawyers.*

Surrogacy: A legal and practical guide for Queensland is Elizabeth's fifth book.

You can contact Elizabeth at her offices as follows:

Phone: 07 3343 9522
Email: mail@lifelaw.com.au
Web: www.lifelaw.com.au
LinkedIn: @elizabethfairon

Made in the USA
Monee, IL
04 November 2026

67385883R00069